THE GLORIOUS DAYS OF

MUSIC HALL &
VARIETY THEATRE

IN KENT'S SEASIDE RESORTS

BY
MICHAEL FAIRLEY

First published 2022

Mifair Publishing – Potters Bar, Herts, England

ISBN 978-0-9543967-7-0

Typeset in Times 11pt on 18pt

Design by Concept Design

Printed by Kindle Direct Publishing, an Amazon .com company

THE GLORIOUS DAYS OF

MUSIC HALL & VARIETY THEATRE

IN KENT'S SEASIDE RESORTS

BY
MICHAEL FAIRLEY

Dedication

This book is dedicated to my grandfather, Charles Kay, comedian, actor and popular music hall and variety artist in England and Scotland during the first two decades of the 20th century. He was well-loved by Kent seaside audiences and was a regular and well-encored performer at many of the county's coastal theatres.

Sadly he died many years before I was born, but I did manage to document his life story, published as 'One of life's great charmers – a biography of Charles Kay' in 2017. This looks at his life as a sporting legend, an Olympic gold medallist, and as a songwriter, comedian and radio presenter.

This new book is more specifically dedicated to the years he spent touring Kent's music halls and theatres, their history, and to documenting some of the many artistes and acts that performed in them over the years.

Foreword

Charles Kay was a comedian, song writer, actor, sketch writer and pantomime villain who performed at music halls and variety theatres across London, in large provincial towns and cities, and around many of England's coastal towns. In particular, he was a firm, popular, and regular entertainer at more than a dozen of Kent's seaside resorts – from Sheerness, around the coast to Seasalter, Whitstable, Herne Bay, Ramsgate, Deal, Dover, Folkestone, Sandgate and then Lydd, during the period from 1906 to 1920.

Although the main coastal towns such a Folkestone, Ramsgate, Margate and Sheerness were able to attract, and pay, many of the best national and international stars that could fill 1,000 - 2,000 seat halls, many of them often having a history dating back to the 1860s, 1870s and 1880s, the smaller Kent seaside venues had their own touring acts that moved from town to town around the coast, often supplemented by well-know local entertainers. Some performers might have been lucky enough to be booked for a whole summer season.

Between these two different types of venues, there were literally hundreds of lesser-known or very specialized performers and acts (both human and animal) of almost infinite variety that often moved twice a week from theatre to theatre throughout the summer season and, for some, the added bonus of winter tours and the annual Christmas pantomimes.

By the first couple of decades of the 1900s, halls and theatres in Kent coastal towns were beginning to be adapted to additionally encompass the new world of moving pictures – initially black and white and silent films, and then sound and big-budget colour films and musicals – while new halls designed for both variety theatre and cinema (commonly called cine-variety) started being built around the Kent coastal towns prior to 1910.

Charles Kay was fortunate (or talented) enough to play at both large and small venues in Kent, and often put together and managed his own touring vaudeville shows and pantomime productions. This book presents the results of extensive historical research and documents the history of many of the Kent music hall and variety theatres that Charles Kay performed at around the county's coast, how they evolved and eventually adapted to a new world of cinema, dance and big bands, as well as documenting much of the rich variety of human and animal acts that delighted audiences in these big and small venues.

Sadly, almost all of the theatres and halls that Charles Kay performed at around Kent's coast in the early 1900s have now been demolished and rebuilt as shops, offices or apartments, and little seems to have been previously well-documented about their long history, or the music hall and variety artistes and speciality acts that performed in them.

Researching these halls and theatres, and the varied artistes that toured them, has entailed many hours of searching through probably a thousand or more historic Kent newspaper show reports and theatre advertisements which are all available on-line through the British Newspaper Archive, as well as many theatre and music hall archives, photo libraries and specialised theatre, cinema, and other web sites. It has been an interesting project, and fascinating to read about both theatre history and the numerous performers and acts – including many that would be frowned on today, or would not even be bookable in theatres in the 21st century. Times are very different, but it should be remembered that music hall and variety theatre gave successful employment to thousands of performers, many of them very highly paid, for around 80 to 100 years, and gave joyful entertainment to millions of England's population.

It is hoped that readers of this book will be equally fascinated and interested to learn and understand more about Kent's coastal music hall and theatre venues, and those artistes and acts – like Charles Kay – that performed on the county's stages as a living.

Michael Fairley

Contents

KENT'S GOLDEN AGE OF MUSIC HALL AND VARIETY THEATRE

Long before the Kent seaside became a home for music hall and variety theatre it was already becoming a fashionable place to visit. Within easy travelling distance – by the earlier 19th century steamship companies and then, a little later, on paddle steamer excursions – from London and the Medway towns, the seaside towns of Sheerness, Whitstable, Herne Bay, Margate, Ramsgate, Deal and Folkestone were a great attraction for a day out and some sea bathing. Indeed, Margate and Ramsgate had already become well established as coastal sea bathing resorts long before 1800.

Documentation from Ramsgate as far back as the 1750s talks about the use of bathing machines fitted with canopies which could be moved forward on wheels, lowering the machine into the sea to enable bathers to enter the water and bathe in complete privacy.

Piers to accommodate the steamship day trippers were built at Sheerness, Herne Bay and Deal in the 1830s, at Margate in the 1850s, Dover in the 1880s, and Folkestone's Victoria Pier in the 1890s. These piers became the fashionable places to promenade and, as the seaside attractions continued to grow during the second half of the 19th century, the pier companies went on to develop their own pier attractions by adding pavilions (Herne Bay, Margate, Folkestone and Dover) or a theatre (Herne Bay), and providing entertainment such as, concerts, plays, variety acts, tram rides, dancing and bands, as well as stalls, amusement machines and tearooms.

In their aim to provide the best seaside experience, Kent's seaside resorts vied with each other to have the best pier, the most unique

1

Herne Bay Pier and Tram believed to be photographed circa 1900

attraction, the best entertainment, or the best holiday experience. The piers, boarding houses, landladies, and donkey rides provided an escape for a population largely housed in the City and more industrialised towns and looking for more freedom – and fun. However, the steamers only had the seaside business to themselves for a relatively short period until the railways began extending their routes into Kent's main coastal towns during the period from 1840 to 1860.

By then the first cross channel passenger steamers were already operating, more passengers were crossing in each direction – for both business and pleasure – and the economic benefits of Dover to Calais ferries continued to grow. Bigger and better ferries and rising demand in the second half of the 19th century meant that by the late 1800s port facilities on both sides of the channel needed to be improved and expanded.

The Quayside and Harbour at Ramsgate in the early 1900s

During this time rail lines from London to Folkestone and Dover were completed and opened in 1844, with a branch line extending down to Folkestone Harbour and described as one of the steepest railway lines in the country. The first rail lines to Ramsgate and Margate followed in 1847. Lines were then added from Faversham to Whitstable and Herne Bay in the 1860s, as well as from Sittingbourne to Sheerness, also during the 1860s.

Kent's seaside resorts were now fully opened to visitors from across Kent and London. King George IV had already patronised Ramsgate in the 1820s, while Folkestone grew so rapidly that it was to be described as one of England's most fashionable coastal towns of the time during the late Victorian and then Edwardian era and was also visited by Royalties - amongst them Queen Victoria and Edward VII and his mistress Alice Keppel (who regularly enjoyed the luxury, and discretion, of the Grand Hotel on the Leas) as well as other members of the English Aristocracy. It also helped that an integrated rail and ferry service from London to Paris, via Folkestone and Boulogne, had been opened in 1849.

By 1900, there were some four steamship companies running twice daily return sailings between Ramsgate and London, calling variously at Margate, Herne Bay, Sheerness, Southend, London Bridge, Greenwich and Woolwich, as well as twice daily steamship services between Ramsgate, Deal and Folkestone, and cross-channel ferries to Calais, Boulogne and Ostend. Other steamships operated from Strood Pier to some of Kent's coastal towns.

One of the small paddle steamers that plied the Thames and Kent coastal resorts in 19th Century

It is perhaps not surprising then, that with fashionable London society and the new, more affluent working class, travelling across the channel, on seaside excursions from London by steamer and rail, and then looking to stay in the boarding house and hotels, that they also wanted to experience in Kent's coastal towns what they were becoming used to and expected in London – music halls and then from the mid 1880s, the variety theatres that started succeeding them. These were now fast becoming one of the most popular forms of affordable entertainment for theatre and musical acts in Britain. Attractions that were to last for something like sixty to seventy years.

A DIVERSE RANGE OF PERFORMERS

The second half of the 19th century saw members of the public flocking in large numbers to halls and theatres in towns, cities and the fast growing seaside resorts all around the country to sing along or join in with favourite (often bawdy, lewd or scandalous) popular songs and verses – such as 'Piddlin' Pete', 'The Farting Contest' or 'The Bell-Ringer's Daughter' of the time, or watch entertainments as wildly diverse as acrobats, jugglers, trapeze artists, burlesque dancers, comedians, hypnotists, wire walkers, ladder balancers, stick manipulators, door and umbrella spinners, mind readers, conjurors and magicians, ventriloquists, butterfly fanners, clog and sand dancers, contortionists and mimics. All these entertainers can be found by perusing the various newspaper advertised programmes from halls and theatres around the Kent coast.

In addition, on these same programmes there were also a whole range of speciality acts such as Russian Cossack dancers, a one-legged comedian, can-can dancers, operatic and ballet selections, Singing Blacksmiths, Long Boot Dancing, "Athelda" a Lady Champion Strong Act, 'The Freaks,' all kinds of athletic artists, 'black-face minstrels,' marionettes, and even singing minstrel troupes and dancers, various negro (billed as freed American slaves) or 'Coon' turns, plus midgets and dwarfs.

Perhaps an interesting example of the diverse range of music hall performers' was Little Dando, a quaint little figure who was promoted as one of the smallest comedians in the world. He was said to "look under 4ft., but appearances are deceptive, and he may be quite that height." Dando appeared in several roles at Sandgate's Alhambra Theatre of Varieties, his favourite ones being as a policeman and a highland laddie. He looked well in kilts, but was more laughed at than admired, his business, of course, being to create amusement. He was one of the most popular "turns" in programmes, and there were generally big houses to see him perform.

All kinds of animals could be found appearing around the county's music halls: acrobatic dogs, dancing dogs, boxing dogs and cats, a "talking" horse, a trick pony, performing rabbits, a horse that was good at arithmetic and could play whist, "Tomato" the Educated Donkey, "Ginger" the Trained Donkey; highly trained pigeons, Techow's Cats, Corbyn's Dogs, an elephant, a lion, and juggling sea-lions. A popular top of the bill act was "Liege's Monkey Hippodrome," in which every part was played by a monkey, including the orchestra – with the monkeys between them playing every musical instrument.

There was also "Maude Rochez's performing monkeys," and

Leoni Clarke extravagant animal acts in which a monkey played a mandoline, a cat performed with a whistle, and a rabbit banging a tambourine. Marvellous performing parrots driving a car, riding a tricycle and a swing were presented by Mons. Roelgin.

By 1914 all kinds of new age acts had started to appear, such as roller skating, trick cyclists; 'The Hall and Wilson Trio' as the Great Motorcycling Sensation; "Yuma, the automaton," The Langfords, with 'Lightning through Transmitters;' Jack G. Silvano, the Comedy Cyclist; a Globe Walker, and Tom Wheatley, the 'Original Railway Ventriloquist' – with his own Railway Station stage set, Burlesque Engine and effects.

Performers were often quite young when they first took to the stage, some only in their very early teens. Indeed, one of the country's greatest-ever music hall stars, Marie Lloyd, was just 14 when she first appeared. Over the years her ability to add lewdness to the most innocent of lyrics of songs such as 'A Little of What you Fancy' or her song with the lyric 'I sits among the cabbages and peas' created clashes with many of the country's guardians of morality – but she was widely applauded during her several visits to Margate, Sheerness and Folkestone's theatres.

Limericks were sometimes brought into performances as recitations. An example might be:

King Richard, in one of his rages,
Forsook his good lady for ages,
He rested in bed,
With a good book instead,
Or, preferably, one of his pages.

Many of the diverse music hall and variety performances and songs of the late 1800s and early 1900s would undoubtedly not be acceptable in the 21st century, yet they provided employment for literally thousands of travelling performers and speciality acts, as well as all the hall and theatre, stage, scenery and management employees necessary to make the shows take place and provide refreshments and drinks.

MUSIC HALL AND VARIETY EVOLVE

Commencing, and thriving as a cultural phenomenon, in the early Victorian era beginning around 1850, and extending through the Edwardian period of British history between 1901 to 1910, and then largely surviving through the First World War, the early music halls and variety theatres evolved from concert, song and supper room establishments during the 1830s, 1840s and 1850s.

In 1899, the largest British chain of variety theatres and music halls was created with the merger of the theatre companies owned by Sir Edward Moss, Richard Thornton and Sir Oswald Stoll in 1899 – Moss Empires. The business was very successful, with major variety theatres in almost every city in Great Britain and Ireland, and was to become advertised as the largest theatre group in the world.

The company placed advertisements in the theatre newspapers each week to show their contracted artists which theatre they were performing at during the following week. The adverts also stated that artists must have band parts prepared for at least twelve different instruments for the orchestras. It further stated that artists must forward copies of songs to the Stage Department at the Stoll Moss corporate

*Moss Empires placed an advertisement in the main theatre
newspapers each week to show their contracted artists where they
were due to be performing during the following week.*

offices in London two weeks before their stage opening performance, while asking artists to note carefully that their contract clause relating to being present for rehearsals would be strictly enforced.

Many of the country's hundreds of early music halls, variety theatres and concert venues can be traced back to the entertainment provided in London's 18th and 19th century coffee houses and taverns in which professional or amateur performers would sing songs while customers, who would be eating and drinking, joined in with the singing or informal entertainment. These gatherings became so popular that the 'entertainment' became more formalised over several evenings a week, often until the early hours of the next morning.

It was said that the taverns, saloons and supper rooms would have been noisy and quite difficult places in which to perform. The audience would talk and shout out throughout the various acts and could be very boisterous and rowdy, even to the extent of throwing things at the performers, such as beer bottles, old boots and, it's said, even dead cats.

PURPOSE-BUILT HALLS AND THEATRES COME TO THE SEASIDE RESORTS OF KENT

Purpose-built music halls in London, some quite ornate, had begun to appear in the early 1850s, being built on, or in, the grounds of some or the more popular beer-houses, taverns or hotels. It was not long before these purpose-built music halls started spreading beyond London to other towns and then to the fast-growing mid, and late 19th century, fashionable seaside resorts in Kent.

This was certainly the origin of the Alexandra Music Hall in Sandgate, Kent, which evolved from a concert room and music hall on the back of a local beer-house in 1858 and later (in 1890) being renovated and refurbished as a six hundred seat theatre and changing its name to the New Alhambra Palace of Varieties. It was described at its re-opening as "a select place of entertainment, where a man might bring his wife, his sister, or his sweetheart." The theatre closed in 1914, later becoming the Rex Cinema.

In nearby Folkestone, The Pleasure Gardens Theatre had opened just a few years earlier in 1886, on a site where it had previously been constructed as an Exhibition Hall. Like many of Kent's other theatre and concert venues it was to later be converted into a cinema before closing its doors in 1964 and eventually being demolished.

Sheerness built its own music hall, drama, concert and entertainment venue on the corner of the Broadway during 1869, opening the doors to the brand new 1,200 seat Victoria Hall in January 1870. this variously changed its name over the years to the Victoria Hall Theatre, the Royal Victoria Theatre, the New Victoria Theatre and, eventually becoming the Hippodrome Cinema.

Other music hall and variety theatres developed out of the circus and performances with horses. Hence the name Hippodrome that initially came to be used for some of the other venues. In Kent for example, the Royal Palace Theatre, Ramsgate, started its early life when George Sanger built Sanger's Amphitheatre as a circus building in 1883 that included housing for performing horses. The building then also found use in the town for the presentation of opera and drama performances.

A major conversion followed in 1908. This converted building had a quite striking exterior with, internally, boxes and two balconies, and became known as the Royal Palace Theatre. In 1911 it presented the 'Babes in the Wood' pantomime. This was said to be the largest touring pantomime in Kent, with the number of performing artists numbering upwards of 60 – including no less than forty London dancers. The theatre was to close in 1960.

Still in Ramsgate and on the horse theme, The King's Theatre, which was opened in 1910, was built on the site of the Red Lion livery stables and located in the narrow Kings Place, off of King Street. It also housed a spacious cinema. Entrance to the theatre was through a tiny foyer at street level. A particularly interesting feature at the rear of the auditorium were some six stained glass windows.

Just around the coast, the Margate Hippodrome opened its doors in 1898, and was originally called The New Grand Theatre. The new building incorporated four walls from the former Royal Assembly Rooms that had been on the site – which had burnt down in 1882. One of the country's biggest music hall stars, Marie Lloyd, was to take part in a concert at the Hippodrome in the early part of the 1900s.

As mentioned earlier, some of Kent's piers, such as those at Margate, Herne Bay, Folkestone and Dover added 'pavilion' extensions and constructions that were used for entertainment that included concerts, variety acts, dancing, bands, and even wrestling or roller skating.

It was not only piers where pavilions were to become established. The Lawn Pavilion at Tankerton started life as an open air stage on grass slopes until eventually a single story building was constructed on the site. This was primarily a theatre for small variety productions and concerts and was known as the New Pavilion.

Whitstable and Tankerton at this time was said to be one of the most popular resorts on the Kent coast. Apart from the New Pavilion in Tankerton, the Whitstable and Herne Bay Assembly Halls were also used for concert and variety shows, while nearby Seasalter even held regular variety performances and concerts in the Seasalter Parish Hall. Faversham used a nearby converted school building, and later, a cinema – where a comedian would come on stage while the films were being changed over.

BY POPULAR REQUEST

How do we know all of this? They were all venues played by Charles Kay, comedian, singer and songwriter, actor, theatre and pantomime producer. Charles Kay, the son of a vicar and, later, a successful sportsman who played rugby, hockey and cricket at County level for Devon and then captained an England cricket team that won a gold medal at the 1900 Paris Olympics, was a regular and popular performer in all these Kent seaside towns. The *Whitstable Times and Herne Bay Herald* of 19th December 1908, described him as "decidedly one of the most popular comedians who has ever visited Whitstable proving to be the 'star' turn".

Looking at the rich variety of programmes displayed by Kent's music halls and variety theatres and performers, including Charles Kay, many of the acts appeared at a particular venue "by popular request" year after year, and then frequently moving around the other Kent coastal

Charles Kay in character in his skit, "Detective Copp"

13

venues during the summer season, appearing for a few days or weeks at each. Christmas time, and many of the regular summer entertainers (again Charles Kay) now popped up again in the various seaside pantomimes as principal boys or girls, or as the villains, robbers, wicked fairies or uncles. But more of Charles Kay later.

Many of the new pavilion and music hall establishments all around the country and at Kent's seaside resorts were distinguished from established theatres of the time by the fact that in a music hall environment you would generally be seated at a table in the auditorium and could drink alcohol and smoke tobacco whilst watching the show. In a theatre, by contrast, the audience was seated in stalls or up in a balcony, and there was a separate bar-room. The acts were loudly applauded. Fun, frolic, good singing, and plenty of comic incidents were conspicuous features in all these well ordered entertainments. Having said that, it could often be a quite rowdy experience, but it appealed to all those who wanted to join in an evening of frivolity and raucous fun.

Although music halls were predominately a feature of the Victorian era, they still had a place after the Queen's death in 1901, and then into Edwardian England, although by 1910 many halls were also starting to show the early generations of black-and-white silent and, later, the early talking colour films' or rebranding their entertainment as variety – or a combination of both, which adopted the name cine-variety.

It is perhaps also worth mentioning that, following Queen Victoria's death on the 22nd January 1901, most public engagements and entertainments were abandoned as a mark of respect, while theatres and music halls decided to temporarily close, again as a show of respect for the Queen.

As far as the standard and quality of musical performances in Kent's music halls is concerned, a presentation by the Archdeacon of Maidstone, the Ven. H. Maxwell Spooner, during the opening of the Sidney Cooper School of Art, Canterbury, on Friday 22nd December 1911, perhaps provides an interesting perspective. In his talk to the students the Archdeacon discussed the nation's love of music, commenting that "it used to be said that England was singularly devoid of appreciation of music." "This," he said, "was improving, but not up to the standard one found when they went abroad and found people assembled in large numbers to listen to lengthy concerts."

"Fortunately," he said, "abroad the concerts were generally given out of doors and not in stuffy rooms as was often the case in England. Abroad they found large audiences enjoying music that was definitely not of the kind found at English music halls. On the continent they really enjoyed good music."

It was the advent of World War I that provided something of a resurgence in the popularity of the music hall and variety theatre, with many singing performances – and music and song composers – wholeheartedly throwing themselves into rallying public support and enthusiasm for the war effort. Music hall audiences enthusiastically joined in with the leading patriotic music hall compositions such as "Keep the Home Fires Burning" , "Pack up Your Troubles" , "It's a Long Way to Tipperary" and "We Don't Want to Lose You (but we think you ought to Go)".

Music hall and variety entertainment continued during the period between the first and second World Wars, but was now no longer the single dominant form of popular entertainment in Britain. The building of purpose-built cinemas – including those in many of Kent's seaside resorts – and improvements in film production and content, together with the continued development of radio, and cheaper and better manufacturing of the gramophone player and recordings meant that the popularity of music halls now declined greatly. Sadly, many of Kent's seaside music hall, pavilion and variety theatre venues were eventually to be demolished.

Music hall and variety entertainment also had to compete with a new era of jazz, swing and big band dance music that sprung up in halls around the country, with well-known bands such as Jack Hylton and Billy Cotton making visits to the Kent coastal halls and

Billy Cotton and his Orchestra visited Folkestone in the 1930s

NEXT WEEK:
"Red Hot and Blue Moments"

CHOCOLATES, CIGARETTES and ICES
can be obtained from the Attendants.

★ **ALL STAR VARIETY** ★

𝕻rogramme

A Bell will be rung in the Bars One Minute before commencing

1. Overture
2. The Dolly Girls & Ethel
   On with the dance.
3. Billy Kray & Margi Morris
   The Popular Revue Comedian
4. Avlis and Francis
   Strings and Steps
5. Eddy Bayes
   The Radio Gangster
6. Hamilton Conrad's Pigeons
   The Prettiest Act in Vaudeville
7. Interval

Selection—"On With the Show" ... H. Nicholls
By the Palace Theatre Orchestra
(Under the direction of Mr. FRANK WALLER)

A Bell will be rung in the Bars One Minute before the next Act

8. The Four Dolly Girls & Ethel
   Again Dance
9. Billy Kray & Margi Morris
   Will Again Entertain
10. Iris Saddler
    The New Star Comedienne
11. Pat O'Brien
    The Irish Street Singer of B.B.C. Fame

Programme subject to slight alteration.

12. Bennett and Williams
    The Famous Radio Phono-Fiddle Comedians
13. Finale
    By entire Company

GOD SAVE THE KING.

Although this is not a CONTINUOUS PERFORMANCE patrons arriving late may enter providing SEATS ARE AVAILABLE and remain to see the whole programme.

During the Interval don't fail to visit our WELL-APPOINTED LOUNGE BARS. Beers, Wines and Spirits at Popular Prices

All Star Variety Programme from the Palace Theatre, Ramsgate, for Monday 1st August, 1938

theatres. New licensing restrictions also had an impact on the character of the halls.

With the ending of the second World War, the era of music halls and variety theatres in the country, and in Kent's coastal resorts, was on the wane and was beginning to steadily fade away to be replaced by cinemas and cine-variety halls showing a mix of films and variety entertainment. Some theatres were still presenting "All Star Variety programmes" into the late 1930 and 1940 years, but these were increasingly few and far between.

Having said that the Palace Theatre in Ramsgate continued with variety performances throughout the 1950s, bringing in stars such as Max Miller, Wee Georgie Wood, Monsewer Eddie Gray, Chesney

Allen and Dr Crock (the Mad Musician) and his Crackpots until, in 1960, planning permission was given to convert the Theatre into a retail store.

Some of the music hall performers (like Charles Kay) managed to continue their acts for a few more years by moving to South Africa, or Australia and New Zealand. Some of the leading comedians and singers also managed to get into the new world of radio, films or recording, but for most of the speciality acts there was little further opportunity.

Sadly, most of the music hall and variety theatre venues around Kent's coastline also faded away and have today largely been demolished and rebuilt as housing developments, offices or supermarket shops.

MUSIC HALL AND VARIETY ARTISTS AT KENT'S SEASIDE RESORTS

From what was already known and from further searching of archived Kent newspapers and the various stage and variety papers, Charles Kay, the comedian, is known to have played to audiences at more than sixteen of the county's different seaside halls, theatres and pavilions over many years. It's likely that, in addition to these, there were at least another dozen or so Kent coastal venues putting on music hall, concert or variety entertainments most weeks during the late 1800s and the first fifteen to twenty years of the 1900s.

When it is then considered that many of these venues would change their programmes twice a week – running from, say, Monday to Wednesday, and then Thursday to Saturday, with perhaps even a big band or military concert on the Sunday – then there were a great many acts to be signed by hall managers, and many posters or newspaper advertisements to be almost continuously prepared.

Each programme at each venue would usually be made up of possibly six to twelve or more different acts, some of which – such as dance troupes, acrobats, musical ensembles and singers – could consist of perhaps six, eight, ten or more performers in the troupe, then it can easily be worked out that upwards of 200 or more different acts would be moving around the Kent coastal resorts once or twice each week – particular during the summer holiday season. And that's not counting all the dog, cat, rabbit, pigeon, or horse and donkey performing animals that needed to also be moved around.

During December and January each year, even up to March in some years, some of the bigger resort venues would put on a pantomime containing perhaps a cast of maybe thirty or forty, from the Principal Boy, Dame and Wicked Uncle leads down to the chorus line. These pantomimes often spent a week at each venue, and then moving on to the next town. A touring cast that again was constantly moving around the coastal resorts.

Put all of this together, and it can be deduced that during any one year there were some several hundreds of performing acts – from the top of the Bill stars down to the more lowly bottom of the Bill supporting acts – that needed to be signed, transported, boarded, promoted, rehearsed and organised on a continuous basis. In the case of some the major London and big city stars, such as Marie Lloyd or Lillie Langtry, that came to Kent's seaside resorts, there might even have been the need for a police presence or police escort because of the crowds that came to see them arrive and perform.

Having said that, it was not often that the big music hall and variety artistes could be attracted to Kent. Only a few of these big performers and personalities were to be presented to the county's seaside audiences. Stars such as Marie Lloyd, Dan Leno, Harry Randall, Lillie Langtry, Kitty Loftus or Maud Allen – all of which performed at Folkestone's Victoria Pier or the Pleasure Gardens Theatre during the late 1800s and early 1900s. So what did these top billing artistes bring to Kent's coastal resorts? Let's just take a look at these leading star's performances that made them an attractive audience draw.

MISS MARIE LLOYD

Marie Lloyd was undoubtedly one of the country's biggest music hall stars of the late 1800s and early 1900s, and was a firm favourite of audiences wherever she appeared. She was famous for her trademark quick wit and the parasol she used in her act, as well as for her singing voice, good humour and the personality that she brought to her theatre performances. The way she sang and presented her songs on stage was considered by many to be too saucy, with songs such as 'Every little movement has a meaning of its own,' 'A little of what you fancy does you good,' 'The Piccadilly trot.'

Marie Lloyd, who first appeared at Folkestone's Victoria Pier Theatre in 1898

Marie Lloyd first appeared at the Victoria Pier, Folkestone, in 1898, where she also supported a Cafe Chantant charity event at Strode Park, Herne, to help raise funds on behalf of the Herne Bay Cottage Hospital. The *Folkestone, Hythe, Sandgate & Cheriton Herald* of Saturday 17 September, 1898, reported that the entrance of Marie Lloyd was the signal for a loud outburst of applause. Her first song which found great favour with her audiences, in which she told them of the various things "she would like to try" was followed by her popular effort "The Barmaid." A third song was vociferously demanded and acceded to which touched on the question of mixed bathing, in which, by the way, she could see no harm.'

She also appeared at the Margate Hippodrome – which coincided with a Bank Holiday – where, with undiminished popularity and a clamorous 'Full House' crowd, she held her place in the affections of the public. Reports of the concert said that 'with characteristic candour and charm the comedienne gave of her best, and received a right royal welcome.'

DAN LENO

Mr. Dan Leno, England's funniest comedian, who appeared at Folkestone's Victoria Pier Theatre in 1898 and again in 1904

Said to be the funniest man on the English stage, and certainly at the head of his profession, Dan Leno was a major music hall star of the 1890s, being widely promoted as 'The Funniest Man of Earth.' Famous for his pantomime-style performances. He can also be remembered for being the first and the only 'music hall' performer to fulfil a Royal Command – at Sandringham in 1903.

He first appeared in Folkestone in 1898 and was on the same Bill as Marie Lloyd, as well as appearing with her at the Cafe Chantant charity fund raising event mentioned earlier at Strode Park, Herne Bay. In reporting on the event, the local newspapers commented that 'Dan Leno held the stage and fairly convulsed his audience with his first item "It tickled her," the patter for this being considered exceptionally funny.'

Reports also commented that 'It goes without saying that Dan Leno is an exceptionally good artist because he understands the art of selection, and, inferentially the art of rejection. Take his next songs about "Jim" and "If he won't marry me, I'll marry him." You only have to look at the fun he gets from the flowers in his bonnet.'

His next appearance at Folkestone was at the Victoria Pier in July 1904, where he gave selections from his repertoire at two concerts. Treated as a Drury Lane celebrity, he stayed at the Wampach Hotel and was surrounded by admirers whenever he ventured out. The *Folkestone, Hythe, Sandgate & Cheriton Herald* of the 16th July, 1904, wrote 'From his extensive repertoire he selected two popular items, both of which he gave in admirable style. At his humorous patter the audience roared with laughter. Particularly successful was "Am I the landlord, or am I not?" This fairly brought down the house, according the comedian vociferous applause.'

Dan Leno was undoubtedly the most famous comedian of his generation. Prices for a seat in the stalls at the concerts were five shillings; in the balcony one shilling. His surviving records bear testimony to his drole sense of humour.

Sadly, he died of heart failure at his residence in Clapham Park just a few months later.

HARRY RANDALL

Harry Randall was a leading English comic actor in the late 1800s and early 1900s and, like Dan Leno – his great personal friend – became a very popular pantomime dame. He performed on the Victoria Pier stage in Folkestone a number of times. In his first appearance at the Pier in 1901, he was described as the world-renowned comedian.

In August, 1904, Harry Randall gave two special concerts at Victoria Pier, Folkestone, being recorded a very enthusiastic reception. He was reported as being 'in fine form', and the selections from his repertoire were well chosen. His first song, "Not a Bad Sort Now," created roars of laughter. In response to the vociferous applause he contributed a song telling of experiences in a boarding-house by the sea and this, too, was highly diverting. At his subsequent appearance Mr. Randall was equally successful, his items being received with many demonstrations of delight by the audience, who thoroughly appreciated the favourite comedian.'

Harry Randall subsequently again appeared at Victoria Pier in July 1905. Once again there was a large and enthusiastic audience and his turn posted loud applause. The *Folkestone, Hythe, Sandgate & Cheriton Herald* of Saturday 29th July, 1905, wrote that 'After a few moments the appearance of the noted comedian as "The Plumber" created fresh outburst, and as he sang of thrilling experiences at "ninepencehalfpenny an hour" there was not a grave face in the audience. He was in great form, and at the conclusion of the song the building rang with loud applause.'

His last appearance at the Victoria Pier, Folkestone, was in July 1906.

KITTY LOFTUS

Kitty Loftus, an English dancer, singer and actor-manager, visited Folkestone's Pleasure Gardens Theatre twice during 1903, firstly in the April and then again in November. A leading soubrette of the 1890s and 1900s in comedies, burlesque, pantomime and musical plays, the talented and sprightly comedienne played a flying visit to the Theatre in April 1903 with a full complement of fifty artistes to present the popular musical comedy, "Naughty Nancy" – with Miss Kitty Lofthus in the title role – which had been played by them with so much success at the Savoy Theatre in the summer of 1902. The *Folkestone Express, Sandgate, Shorncliffe & Hythe Advertiser* of Saturday 11th April, 1903, reported that 'it was an expensive undertaking to bring down so large a company for one performance, but Miss Loftus' great popularity will ensure a packed house, and it is advisable for townspeople to make early application for seats before the rush of visitors commences.'

Kitty Lofthus again appeared at the Pleasure Gardens, Folkestone, in November, 1903, in a comedy in three sets entitled 'A Maid From School.' It was described as a very lively play.

MAUD ALLEN

Maud Allan, who appeared at the Victoria Pier, Folkestone, on 7th September, 1909, was a Canadian dancer who had become particularly famous (even notorious) for her Dance of the Seven Veils. This visit to the town was for one of 250 performance she gave in England in under one year, and which made her the highest paid dancer of the time. She was frequently billed as "The Salomé Dancer".

25

Miss Maud Allan famous for her "Salome" dance

Her forthcoming appearance in Folkestone promoted a lengthy report in the *Folkestone Express, Sandgate, Shorncliffe & Hythe Advertiser* of 28th August, 1909, which stated that 'Miss Maud Allan, the young Canadian, who has captivated London with her wonderful classical dancing, will appear at the Pier Pavilion on September 7th for one matinee performance. Not within the history of the present generation has any artiste on the stage created such a spontaneous chorus of praise from the Press and public as has Miss Maud Allan.'

Later in the press report it went on to add that the reason for her success 'was not hard to find. Miss Allan, in her dancing, or series of "musical impressions," has elevated the art of terpsichore to a degree that has never been anticipated by any of its professors or students. It seems generally accepted that Miss Allan is the finished product of a continental school of dancing. This is not so. The artiste has never received a dancing lesson during the whole course of her career.'

26

LILLIE LANGTRY

It was said that 'every one was infected with the hi–larious, whirlwind manner of clever Lillie Langtry, who seems to possess an amount of vivacity unknown to the ordinary individual.' A comedienne and sprightly dancer, Lillie Langtry appeared at Victoria Pier, Folkestone, in 1906. Her performance in the play 'Between the Night and Light' was said to be roundly booed and she had to be escorted off the Pier by the police, followed by an irate crowd.

Miss Lillie Langtry. Performed at the Victoria Pier Pavilion Theatrein 1906

CLARA BUTT

One of the most popular singers in the early 20th century, Clara Butt – later Dame Clara Butt – was a quite exceptional contralto singer which, together with her commanding personality, led to her being admired by Handel, Edward Elgar and Mendelssohn. She was known for her concert performances of ballads and oratorios and appeared at a Grand Sunday Concert at the Folkestone Pleasure Gardens in January 1917.

SARAH BERNHARDT

Born in France, Sarah Bernhardt, was a French stage actress who was later referred to as "the most famous actress in the history of the world." She made her name as a serious dramatic actress on the stages of Europe in the late 1800s and early 1900s, playing lead parts in acclaimed plays and motion pictures. Indeed, was one of the first actresses to star in motion pictures. It would have been quite an achievement to have her appear at the Folkestone Pleasure Gardens Theatre in 1908, coming direct from the Theatre Sarah Bernhardt, Paris, where she had been performing in "La Dame aux Camelias."

MADGE LESSING

Madge Lessing was a famous London stage comedienne, actress and singer, panto principal boy and postcard beauty of Edwardian musical comedy who had a successful career in the West End in London. She made a very successful flying visit appearance at two concerts at the Victoria Pier Pavilion, Folkestone, in August 1906, receiving a very warm reception. Miss Lessing also appeared on Broadway and made early film performances in Germany.

PAUL CINQUEVALLI

Paul Cinquevalli was a German music hall entertainer whose speciality juggling act made him popular in the English music halls during the 19th and early 20th century. Cinquevalli first appeared in England in 1885 with much success and settled in London, appearing in various circuses, music halls and pantomimes, including an appearance in Whitstable in 1912. He

Paul Cinquevalli, the speciality German juggler

was said to have kept everyone holding their breath as he juggles with billiard balls, cues, and glasses.

ELLA SHIELDS

Ella Shields, who was to appear at the Folkestone Pleasure Gardens Theatre for three nights in 1927, was a music hall singer and male impersonator, who became extremely well-known for her famous signature song, "Burlington Bertie from Bow." This song was an immediate hit and is still popular even today.

ARTHUR ROBERTS

Said to be the Prince of Comedians, Arthur Roberts, supported by a powerful vaudeville company, appeared for three nights and a matinee performance at Ramsgate's Palace Theatre in July 1909, where it was reported that he kept the house in a roar of laughter with his original witticisms and entertaining persona in an amusing sketch between a private detective, his German partner and a hospital nurse entitled "The girl who took the wrong (towing) path." It was said that Arthur Roberts could make a dyspeptic rock with laughter.

CHARLES KAY

Like Dan Leno and Harry Randall, Charles Kay was an actor, much applauded comedic song writer and a successful and popular pantomime dame, who performed at most of London's variety theatres, as well as touring the many Stoll Moss Theatres throughout England and Scotland. He co-managed pantomimes at many venues and successfully appeared as the 'wicked uncle' in a range of

Charles Kay

different and popular pantomimes.

Perhaps not in the same salary league as the country's top stars, he regularly returned to Kent's seaside halls and theatres as 'the town's favourite comedian,' by popular request over many years, appearing at some sixteen of the county's resorts – believed to be more than other comedian of the time. As such, he is accorded a separate chapter of his own

Bringing big name stars to Kent's seaside towns was definitely a big challenge. Many of the coastal venues only had a capacity of up to six or seven hundred seats at most. Few venues were therefore big enough to handle the size of audience needed to support the top artistes' performing fees that, by 1909, often ran into the many hundreds of pounds a week that the top performers were demanding at this time.

A report in the *Folkestone Express, Sandgate, Shorncliffe & Hythe Advertiser* of Wednesday 17 February, 1909, made interesting reading for many in the town. This report, in listing fees paid to top performers said; 'It seems almost incredible that any manager could venture to pay a single performer £800 a week. Yet such is the princely salary received by Mr Harry Lauder. It is more than twice what the late Dan Leno ever earned, and his salary was accounted prodigious.' The report went on to say that 'Miss Marie Lloyd delights her audiences to the tune of £240 a week, while Miss Kitty Loftus has for a period commanded even more. Little Tich has a salary of £500 a week. Miss Maud Allen's success as a dancer has made her, at the rate of £300 a week, the best paid exponent of the Terpsichorian art.'

Looking at these figures (even £100 pounds in 1909 would be the equivalent of just over £12,000 in 2022), it is perhaps not surprising that star turns such as Harry Lauder or Little Tich never made it to any of Kent's seaside venues. Kent venues, however, partly made up for the lack of the big stars by instead hiring some of the country's best performing mimics to sing the popular performers' best songs of the period.

MIMICS AND IMPERSONATORS

This meant that on many Bills there would be names such as Miss Lea Davis, 'a smart mimicry turn who impersonated in voice and manner the following music hall artists: Miss Marie Lloyd, Miss Vesta Tilley, Miss Victoria Monks and Harry Lauder.' She also sang a verse or two of the popular songs performed by these stars. Miss Davis could be found performing her mimicry act at Folkestone's Victoria Pier in 1908.

Also appearing in Folkestone with great effect was Lily Sharplin. The local newspaper said of her 'The theatre management have secured a rare prize. She is a serio comic artiste of exceptional ability, and a better imitator of leading theatrical and music-hall celebrities would be impossible to readily conceive; her imitations of Marie Lloyd, Julia Mackay, Phyllis Rankin, and Vesta Tilley are realistically perfect.'

Performers at Sandgate's Alhambra theatre also included mimics. Lil Elfrida, billed as London's premier mimic, presented excellent imitations of Marie Lloyd at the theatre in 1907. She also appeared at the Palace and Hippodrome, Dover, the same year, again mimicking Marie Lloyd, and also Kate Karney, while back in 1902, Daisy Silcott 'in a charming dress, gives her songs in her own inimitable style.' It was said that 'she has the Marie Lloyd style about her and is a very clever artist.'

Many other similar clever mimics of the leading artists, such as Mr. R. F. Knox, could be picked out of the local newspaper archives. The *Whitstable Time and Herne Bay Herald* of Saturday 10 September, 1904, said of Mr. Knox's appearance at the Assembly

Rooms 'It would hard to equal his impersonations and we venture to think that Dan Leno himself would be deceived, so very life-like is the travesty of this comedian. In fact, all his impersonations are really clever, and encored.'

Interestingly, a number of Marie Lloyds actual siblings were also on the stage and appearing at Kent venues. The *Dover Express* of Friday 31st July, 1908, reported that 'This week's programme at Dover's Royal Hippodrome, is an excellent one, and does the management infinite credit. Miss Daisy Wood, who is the sister of the well known music hall artiste, Miss Marie Lloyd, tops the bill in an exceedingly delightful performance and her reception by the audience is most enthusiastic.' The report went on to say that 'Miss Wood shows herself to be very talented artiste, and her latest successes "The Flip-Flap" and "Splash me" are performed with great effect.'

A few months after Miss Daisy Wood's appearance in Dover, the *Sheerness Times Guardian* of 29th August, 1908, noted that Maud and Sydney Wood, vaudeville artistes, and the brother and sister of Miss Marie Lloyd, were making their last appearance in England at the Sheerness Hippodrome prior to their departure for America. It seems that this was a very talented family.

FROM CLASSICAL DANCE TO HIGH KICKING TROUPES

It was not just singers that topped bills at Kent's coastal venues. Miss Maud Allan, the young Canadian, who had captivated London with her wonderful classical dancing, appeared at Folkestone's crowded Victoria Pier Pavilion on September 7th for one flying visit matinee performance. She appeared in no less than seven dances set to music which included Bach, Peer Gynt, Chopin and Strauss. Her performances created the greatest enthusiasm. It was said that she had attracted more people to theatres than any other artist over the previous twenty years. No wonder she attracted a weekly salary that was more than Marie Lloyd.

Dance stars such as Miss Maud Allan however, were not the staple fare of venues such as Sandgate's Alhambra. Here you were more likely to see a dance troupe such as Violet Gibson's Tudor Girls, who, 'whether dancing collectively or individually, are admirable.' They were on the theatre's bill in May 1908.

Folkestone's Victoria Pier also had its share of dancing performances. In both August and September, 1898, one of the great audience draws on the Bill were Tiller's Troupe of Dancing Girls. The *Folkestone, Hythe, Sandgate & Cheriton Herald* of Saturday 17 September, 1898, reported that 'Their agile movements are only equalled by their charming appearance. The "dear girls" fairly brought down the house. Thoroughly refined, well trained, and happy looking, this troupe should have a welcome wherever it appears.

It was also separately reported in the same newspaper that 'the lively and vivacious eight girls comprising the Tiller Troupe of Imperial Dancers have once more given evidence of their own department in frills, lace, and furbelows. We understand "the girls" have represented England in the art of high kicking on the continent, and have everywhere been received with great enthusiasm.'

Acrobatic and gymnastic performances were also staple fair at many of the Kentish venues. At Victoria Pier, Folkestone in August 1908, Victoria Dagmar gave a very interesting gymnastic display on the horizontal bar and gymnastic rope. The *Folkestone Express, Sandgate, Shorncliffe & Hythe Advertiser* of Saturday 22nd August, 1908, said that 'For a lady, the performance is decidedly clever. She is assisted by her partner, who acts as a clown, and this gentleman creates roars of laughter by his antics.'

Also appearing in Kent at this time were The Kellino Troupe of Acrobats. They consisted of three ladies, three gentlemen, and two boys, and their pyramids, etc, were said to be marvellously well performed.

An example of the kind of diverse and good musical acts that also performed at Victoria Pier and other Kent venues would perhaps be The Frassettis. Between them, they played well on the harp, violin and xylophone with wonderful smartness. Their performances on the xylophone were said to be much commended. The *Folkestone Express, Sandgate, Shorncliffe & Hythe Advertiser* of Saturday 22nd August, 1908, commented 'We are not lovers of musical novelties as a rule, but the xylophone in such capable hands is a delight.'

For sheer novelty on the seaside stage then Miss Belle Green might be worth some consideration. Also appearing on the same Victoria Pier bill as the Frassettis, Miss Belle Green was said to give a most entertaining "turn." Her child mimicry is very smart and she is loudly encored. The amusing way in which she relates the history of England is greatly appreciated. Miss Green tells a few comical stories of English Kings and Queens which the 'chroniclers appear to have overlooked.'

On some of the theatre billings there are artistes names that appear without any explanation of what their acts are about. On the programme at the Alhambra Theatre of Varieties, Sandgate, in November 1902 for example, was the name of 'Fanny Smart.' But what her act was is something of a mystery.

At some of the smaller venues around the coast the list of performers might also include one or more popular local artistes that had obtained popularity and distinction playing the piano, singing well-known songs, or even at mimicking one or more of the country's star turns.

This all made for the rich variety of acts that Kent's coastal towns could offer local and visiting audiences.

CHARLES KAY - KENT'S FAVOURITE SEASIDE COMEDIAN

Charles Kay, comedian, singer and songwriter, actor, and pantomime producer, performed many times on stage at more than sixteen different music, concert hall and variety entertainment venues around the Kent coast – from Sheerness, Faversham, Seasalter, Tankerton, Whitstable and Herne Bay, round to Ramsgate, Deal, Dover, Folkestone, Sandgate and Lydd – from 1905 to 1921, both during the summer season and then bringing pantomime to the resorts during the winter period, returning year after year to venues by popular request.

Perusing newspaper archives from the early 1900s it appears that no other comedian and variety artist had the kind of success in Kent's seaside resorts as Charles Kay. It no doubt helped that he was variously described in *The Stage* newspaper over the years as the possessor of a fine appearance, handsome, charming, charismatic, a real and original comedian of great experience, intensely funny, a popular favourite with young and old, while his character impersonations, particularly clerical imperson_ ations, were described as most

Charles Kay, a popular favourite with Kent's seaside theatre audiences from 1905 to 1921

39

droll. He was certainly popular with the ladies, who often turned out in force for some of his more racy performances.

Further endearing him to the seaside audiences he also participated in local cricket matches, charity and fund raising events, and even organising or judging beauty and baby contests, as reported by the *Whitstable, the Kentish Times and Farmers Gazette* of 3rd October 1908, during the time he was performing for the season in Whitstable. This report stated that 'Charles Kay, the popular comedian and a firm favourite in Whitstable, organised another Beauty and Baby Show in the Assembly Halls. Miss Florence West was chosen as the prettiest girl in Whitstable, receiving a gold bangle. A fine one-year old little girl received a gold brooch. The evening concert included Miss Hirlemann, contributing old favourites. Mr. Charles Kay surpassed himself singing 'Sheltering Tree.'

SUCCESS AS A COMIC SONGWRITER

Many of his performances around the Kent coast were of songs that he had written and composed himself; sometimes to his own music and at other times by taking popular songs of the time and then researching and rewriting different words to reflect current news stories – both local and national – topical events and themes. Initially he was billed as a 'Descriptive Vocalist,' such as when he appeared at the Alhambra Theatre of Varieties, Sandgate, in March 1906.

Two months later *The Era* stage newspaper reported on the crowded opening night of the new Palace of Varieties, Lydd , where Charles Kay, the popular comedian, who performed his topical song, 'The Beautiful Tale of Love.' Then in May 1908, the *Folkestone*

Express, Sandgate, Shorncliffe & Hythe Advertiser reported that at the Alhambra, Sandgate, 'Charles Kay scored greatly with a song of his own composition concerning his "Tobacco Queen." In this song all the different brands of tobacco, cigars and cigarettes - even the famous Woodbines – are noted.

In another newspaper of the time it was said that 'Mr. Charles Kay, the new comedian, makes a most notable success. He assumes the character of a man who sells sheets of songs outside theatres, etc. The ever increasing titles of the ditties he vends induces him to express his views on topical matters in their words. His song, employing the names by which the favourite songs of the moment are known, is cleverly written, and gauges the public taste to a nicety. Mr. Kay has quite a new style, a style which should keep his name permanently on the popular variety programmes.'

This song, which he titled 'A Muddled Melody' proved to be such a success that it was purchased by B Feldman, the London music publisher, and reported widely as 'a great number' and a big success, being sung by performers everywhere on the Stoll Moss circuit. He later wrote and produced a whole show based on the song title which was performed in both the London and Provincial theatre,

At other times he again took events of the day and, rather than writing a song, built them into a skit or sketch, regularly performing them on stage with his current stage assistant or partner as The Typical Topical Talker. This was the case when he was performing at the New Pavilion, Tankerton, in August 1908. Here, the local Whitstable paper commented that 'Large houses were the order of the day. Charles Kay, The Typical Topical Talker is, if possible, now more popular than ever. His parody on the 'Old Apple Tree' is screamingly funny and his references to Tankerton's Dorando (Dorando was an Italian marathon runner who finished first in the 1908 London Olympics, but was later disqualified) and the Slavier Case created quite a furore.

The newspaper also mentioned that 'an excellent portrait of him appeared in last week's "*Throne and Country*," and then mentioned that Mr. Rowland has wisely re-engaged him to return in September when he will be given a complimentary benefit.

As a an excellent baritone singer, many of his performances around Kent's coastal resorts were of the, then, current popular songs. In a concert at the Assembly Rooms, Whitstable in September 1908, Charles Kay sang 'The Beautiful Tale of Love' and when encored gave the audience 'Girls, Girls, Beautiful Girls'. Also on the same programme was Hedda Hirleman who sang 'Pussy had another sardine' at the piano and then rendered a duet with Charles Kay entitled 'Nobody knows, nobody cares'. Both songs were encored. His final song was 'Come and have a drink with me.'

The month before, he was on the bill of fare at the Victoria Pier, Ramsgate, where the entertainment was promoted as 'A French Danselse.' In this commendable enterprise the famous Parisian dancer, Mademoiselle Dory-Ta had been engaged. The *Folkestone Express, Sandgate, Shorncliffe & Hythe Advertiser* of Saturday 22nd August 1908, said that 'Mademoiselle, who possesses a dainty figure and is very graceful, dances in a manner not often seen in this country. The style, however, pleases the audience, who applaud the Parisienne in a warmhearted fashion.

Charles Kay, who was also in the programme gives several capital songs and is well received. On Monday evening he was repeatedly recalled.'

Amongst Charles Kay's regular, songs, skits and sketch performances that he performed around Kent's coastal resorts was that given during another of his regular evenings at the Alhambra, Sandgate. In April 1912, the *Folkestone Express, Sandgate, Shorncliffe & Hythe Advertiser* of Saturday 6 April 1912, noted that 'Charles Kay, comedian, is no stranger, and he was given a reception on Monday night such as is only accorded to established favourites. Charles now appears before the footlights in his Skit entitled 'The Vicar,' the story of a guileless vicar. His success in this role quite puts all previous ones in the shade.'

A number of variations on the vicar theme were also successfully developed by Charles Kay, sometimes calling the skit 'The curate' and on other occasions developing the vicar concept into a song. This was the case when he appeared at the King's Theatre, Ramsgate where, with his partner Lola Trent, they created much merriment and he was warmly applauded for his song "The Vicar of Slopton."

It was perhaps no surprise that he often made fun of vicars and the clergy. His father was the rector of Greatworth, Northamptonshire, and he spent the first ten years of his life listening to his father talking about the church and day-to-day religious life. His father died when he was ten, but his mother then remarried another vicar.

Apart from vicars, another of Kay's very popular skits, which he presented with different partners for many years from 1906 onwards, was entitled 'Detective Copp.' Regularly updated as a story of a

*Charles Kay and Lola Trent (his then wife's stage name)
performing in the skit entitled 'Detective Copp.'*

hapless detective interviewing a young lady, the skit was still being played at the Playhouse, Faversham – where he had gained popularity on previous appearances – as late as December 1918.

PANTOMIME PERFORMER AND PRODUCER

Apart from his success as a comedian, songwriter and popular baritone, Charles Kay, appeared as the Baron in long-running pantomimes in quite a number of major towns and seaside resorts around England. He certainly honed his early pantomime credentials in Kent, initially at the Royal Palace Theatre, Ramsgate, and then at the Hippodrome, Sheerness. In both of these, and at major city and town venues around the country, he performed many times as the Baron Bunkum, the wicked uncle, in Babes in the Wood, which was the premier children's pantomime in the country at this time.

The pantomime at the Royal Palace Theatre, Ramsgate, in January 1911, with Charles Kay as Baron Slopton and Bert Morland as Nurse Prettypot, had come directly from performing at the Woolwich Theatre the week before, and contained no lest than ten effective and artistic scenes. All the dresses had all been specially designed for the production by the following modistes of repute, namely Mesdames Alias, Simmons and Comelli, therefore promising something out of the ordinary. The *East Kent Times and Mail* of Wednesday 11th January 1911, reported that 'a special feature is made of the ballets, for which not less than forty Loudon dancers have been engaged under the direction of Mr. Paul Valentine, the doyen of all our most celebrated masters of the terpsichorean art. He will also be responsible for the production of the pantomime, which is the largest touring, the artists number upwards of 60.'

In March 1912, the same pantomime holds sway at the Hippodrome, Sheerness, but now being presented by Charles Kay and Robert Adams. Described by the *Sheerness Times and Guardian* of Saturday,

Lola Trent as Will Scarlet in "Babes in the Wood"

9th March, 1912, as a 'gorgeous production,' the newspaper continued with 'we are all familiar with the story of Robin Hood and his Merry Men, who discover the Babes after they have been abducted by two ruffians (in the pay of their uncle) to murder them. The story will be closely followed, at the same time plenty of fun will be introduced, for which a special star cast of comedians has been engaged, and once again including Charles Kay and Bert Morland who amused as Baron Slopton and Nurse Prettypot as the dame, with Lola Trent as Will Scarlet. No expense has been spared to make this one of the smartest pantomimes touring, and above all it Is the acme of refinement.'

From his early beginnings both performing in panto and then managing and presenting pantomimes, Charles Kay proved to be a great success over many years in the world of pantomime, playing not only parts such as the Baron Bunkum, but also the Baron in 'Cinderella', Will Atkins in 'Robinson Crusoe' and Abanazar in Aladdin. In 1912 he appeared as the Mayor of Muddleup in 'The House that Jack Built' pantomime at the Theatre Royal Bradford, which ran for nine weeks.

The *Yorkshire Evening Post* stated that Charles Kay as the Mayor was a capital actor of eccentric parts. In addition, The *Halifax Guardian* at that time describes his portrayal of the Mayor of Muddleup as 'leaving nothing to be desired, having a splendid physique, set off to advantage by his splendid mayoral robes.' He also had 15 successful weeks of pantomime at the Princess's Theatre, Glasgow in 1913 and into 1914 and between December 1919 and March 1920 toured with Babes in the Wood playing at Dawlish,

Exeter, Jersey, Guernsey, Bognor, Chichester, Taunton. He was also in the Cinderella pantomime in Bath in 1914.

There can be no doubt that Charles Kay had an important part to play in the evolution and success of the music hall, variety theatre and pantomime in Kent's seaside resorts during the first two decades of the 20th century. His ever popular skits and sketches, his popular songs, comic song writing, and even theatre management and production, had an influence on theatres and halls from Sheerness, all the way round to Lydd, and then beyond Kent to seaside resorts in Sussex, Hampshire, Devon and the Channel Islands.

With the slow demise of variety after the end of World War I, Charles Kay emigrated to Australia in 1921, where he had a further successful six years touring theatres throughout Australia and New Zealand before establishing his own late evening radio show in Melbourne in 1926. Sadly, he died of pneumonia in the city two years later in 1928.

MUSIC HALL AND VARIETY THEATRE ESTABLISHED IN SANDGATE

As a small coastal town sandwiched between Folkestone and Hythe it is perhaps a little surprising to find that one of the first purpose-built music halls around the Kent coastline should have appeared in Sandgate as far back as 1858, when a concert room and music hall were erected on the back of the Bricklayers Arms beerhouse in the town.

After changing the name of the beerhouse to the Alexandra Hotel in 1867 it subsequently ran an advertisement under the name of the Alexandra Music Hall some two years later. Then in 1890, the hotel and music hall was purchased by Thomas Maltby who, according to an October 1890 news feature in the *Folkestone Express, Sandgate, Shorncliffe & Hythe Advertiser*, 'has worked such alterations and changes in the interior of the music hall, that those who knew the old place would not now recognise it, owing to improvements and alterations in which the public comfort and convenience are studied, and the taste for respectable and well conducted variety entertainments.'

The changes referred to in the newspaper included new scenery and an extended stage. The accommodation for the public was also improved, with a large balcony facing the stage. Space in the pit offered nine rows of seats with plenty of room for movement, with the pit stalls separated off by ornamental railing. The whole place was said to be pleasantly decorated by a Mr. Merchant, of the Princess's Theatre, Oxford Street, London.

Lighting in the new theatre was from circular gas lights in the roof and said to give subdued lighting to the auditorium. Much attention was also given to the ventilation arrangements. The newspaper report added that 'space at the disposal of the designer has been made the most of, and, therefore, it was essential that currents of air should constantly pass through the building, and means given for the bloated atmosphere to escape.' Prior to the opening, the magistrates inspected the building structure and gave their approval to all the arrangements and precautions taken for public safety in a building which would often be crowded with large audiences.

This was certainly the case on the opening night when the refurbished music hall and now, a modern variety theatre which could accommodate up to six hundred people, was opened to the public on Monday, November 3rd., 1890, under the name of the New Alhambra Theatre of Varieties, when 'the applause, the expressions of approval, and the excellent entertainment were said to ensure the theatre would have a successful future.'

Amongst the attendance for the opening were a large number of people from Folkestone – representing all classes from Town Councillors, tradesmen, and members of the Masonic body, of which the proprietor, Mr. Maltby, was a member, down to local residents and representatives of the nearby Shorncliffe military establishment. The manner in which they were seated, the comfort, and the character of the refreshments provided, deserved much praise.

During the evening Mr. Maltby, the theatre owner, was called to the front of the stage, and in a few remarks which were loudly applauded, he declared that he 'meant the place to be above all things a select place of entertainment, where a man might bring his wife, his sister, or his sweetheart. The enthusiasm with which this sentiment was received told how much it was reciprocated by the assembled audience.'

The orchestra for the occasion consisted of Mr. Holmans on the piano, and Mr. Hart, on the violin, but, said the *Folkestone Express, Sandgate, Shorncliffe & Hythe Advertiser* in the following week's report 'it is intended in the future to increase this number. Mr. Hart, who so long acted as chairman in the old music hall, resumed that position on this occasion. Mr. J. H. Straight, the experienced manager, provided a variety entertainment for the occasion and the five following nights which, no doubt would have been largely appreciated.'

'As for the entertainment provided, it was a credit to the proprietor, the manager (Mr. Straight), and a forecast of what the public might expect in the future. Mr. Alf Baker and Miss Nellie Beresford in their musical scene " Night Duty " highly amused, Mr. Alf Cawthorn, the vocalist and dancer, delighted the audience with his varieties, and the Sisters Archer as duettists and dancers were excellent. Mr. John Holmes, the negro comedian and bone soloist, caused much fun, as also did Howlett's marionettes.'

Described as an elegant and perfectly appointed Bijou Variety Theatre, the newspaper added that 'As an attempt to provide respectable entertainments for a large number, both of the civil and military element in this neighbourhood, who appreciate music hall entertainments, this deserves to succeed, and, we believe. the proprietor will see a return in popular support for the speculation in which he has so courageously embarked.'

A month after the opening, the *Folkestone Express, Sandgate, Shorncliffe & Hythe Advertiser* reported that 'The New Alhambra Theatre of Varieties maintains the excellent reputation it gained when first opened. The audiences have been most appreciative, and the performances of Frederick and Drew, comedians and dancers, Merry Madge Kellie, serio comic and ballad vocalist, Tom Fancourt, Sailor Baylie, Frank Seymour, and Nellie Cortine, have been loudly applauded. Fun, frolic, good singing. and plenty of comic incidents are conspicuous features in these well ordered entertainments.'

In November 1891 to celebrate their first year, the Alhambra presented a grand anniversary night to celebrate the opening of the Hall under Mr. Thomas Maltby. Long before the performance of the evening commenced the New Alhambra Theatre of Varieties, Sandgate, was crowded, numbers being unable to obtain admission. During the evening Mr. Maltby told the audience that 'during the year there had been abundant evidence that a music hall respectably conducted, on popular lines, was a thing required in the neighbourhood.'

A REGULAR APPRECIATIVE AUDIENCE

The 1890s saw the Alhambra, with its excellent weekly programmes of variety artistes drawn from London, around the south-east of the country, sometimes from across the continent, and also from the wider English music hall scene, bringing in regular appreciative audiences from the Sandgate, Folkestone, Seabrook, Hythe and surrounding area.

The 1892 advertisement shown gives an indication of the mixed programmes of comedians, dancers, singers and speciality acts that the Alhambra regularly provided.

Tom Maltby, the ever-popular proprietor,   relinquished the

Alhambra in March 1907, being succeeded by George Hill, who referred to the Theatre as 'Hill's Hall of Hilarity.' One of Hill's early bookings was James Berry, the hangman, who related quite graphic accounts of how he dispatched his 'clients.'

In the 1901 census it was recorded that The Royal Alhambra Music Hall was at 6 Devonshire Lees, Sandgate. Then in December that year, the Theatre announced that there was now a new entrance to the Stalls in Devonshire Street. It added that the Theatre opened every evening at 7.30 to a 'Magnificent Menu of Mirth.

The Theatre continued to be successful over the following years and always managed to provide an interesting, diverse

MALTBY'S MANSION OF MIRTH.

The
NEW ALHAMBRA,
HIGH STREET, SANDGATE.

Proprietor ... ... Mr. Tom Maltby.
Manager ... ... Mr. Chas. D. Hickman.
(late of Belmont's New Sebright, London.)
MONDAY, MARCH the 29th, AND DURING
THE WEEK.
THE FALCONER SKETCH COMBINA-
TION.
KATE WILLIAMS.
Serio & Dancer.
HARRY BALDWIN
Comedian.
TOPSY LEVANE,
Song and Dance Artiste.
WILL POWELL,
Comedian and Dancer.
SISTERS SLATER,
Duettists and Dancers.
PHIL REYMOND,
The Renowned Vocal Comedian.

Note !
MARCH 31st SPECIAL ENGAGEMENT OF
JOLLY JOHN NASH.

Advertisement in The Folkestone
Chronicle and Advertiser. Saturday
March 5th, 1892. Newspaper image ©
The British Library Board. All rights
reserved. With thanks to
The British Newspaper Archive
(www.britishnewspaperarchive.co.uk)

and well attended weekly programmes. In February 1903 the entertainment included a Romantic Sketch entitled "A White Slave," an Eccentric Comedian, a Conjuror and Humorist, Comedy Sketch Artistes, Prof. Garford and his Troupe of Educated Pigeons (20 in

53

number) and Acrobatic Dogs.

Moving to January 1904, the entertainment included Percy Emery's Sketch Company, a Novel Ventriloquist, a comedienne and Dancer, Comic Entertainers, a Comic Vocalist, a Comedienne and Burlesque Artiste and Instrumentalists. The following month, the Theatre announced it was introducing cake-walk competitions on Thursday and Friday nights. The successful competitor was to be presented with a handsome silver watch (lady's or gent's). A consolation prize would also be awarded, and the judging will be left in the hands of "The Lessors," champion cake walkers, who were appearing nightly.

March 1904 saw a full house for a capital programme. 'All the artistes were enthusiastically received, and in one or two instances encores were demanded. The first to appear was Vera Dalwood, who possessed a fine repertoire of songs, and accomplishes several pleasing dances. She was followed by the Gladwells, a trio who are in every way worthy of the title they have assumed, viz., comic entertainers and general laughter makers.'

Reports about the next performer were not exactly glowing, with one commenting that 'Flo Hastings gave an excellent turn, but having lost the power of her voice, found it difficult to articulate in a manner which captivates the class of audience who assemble at this music hall.

On the same bill were a comic juggler, a duet, and a cosmopolitan mimic, Mr. J. C. Crawley, in which his song "Kilarney" was a feature of his turn, with the programme concluding with a first-class sketch by Miss Beatrice Fielding entitled "At the world's mercy" in which the characters were admirably impersonated.

In August 1904 it was said that the Theatre, now under the energetic management of Mr. G. Leybourne, had become a more popular resort than ever for those who wanted an evening's entertainment. 'Every evening is full houses and the audience express their satisfactions by loud prolonged applause.'

There are three very good "turns" at the Alhambra during the week, reported the local newspaper in May 1906. 'They are given by Harry Wenburn, Ethel Buchanan, and the Davenports. Harry Wenburn is a comedian with plenty of dash and go. His first song, "Funny Little Things," takes well, and "I'll be There" is well received, but " Have a Couple?" is his best and most appreciated effort, as it has a catchy chorus for the audience. Ethel Buchanan is a soprano singer of exceptional merit, and her songs evoke much applause.'

The Davenports were billed as lightning magicians and illusionists, and this description was in no way exaggerated, for the audience were not a little mystified. The male artiste, a very successful card-manipulator, palmed billiard balls in an

Alhambra Poster, June 8th, 1908. Courtesy of the Davenport Collection. www.davenportcollection.co.uk.

astonishing manner. His companion was also clever at similar feats, and between the two a very enjoyable entertainment was given.

The other artistes were also deservedly applauded. Arthur Lomas is in every respect a smart comedian. An excellent evenings entertainment concluded with Payne's biophotoscope. The pictures were humorous and otherwise, and of the latter "An Escape from Sing-Sing Prison" was a most realistic spectacle.

Success for the Alhambra continued unabated. June 1907 sees newspaper reports that included 'In spite of the many counter-attractions, the Alhambra continues to draw crowded audiences nightly. On Tuesday evening the hall was filled to overflowing, and for two hours and a half the patrons enjoyed one of the best entertainments that have been given at the Alhambra for a long time. Variety is the great charm of the programme this week.'

Another report in the same month said that 'There seems to be no limit to the popularity of the Sandgate Alhambra. There are really no slack nights now, a full house being the general run every evening during the week. This week's entertainment offers exceptional attractions, a rattling good programme being submitted. A somewhat novel "turn" is given by a Russian troupe of dancers. Their performance causes more amusement than admiration, and it is funny, it requires no little skill to keep still.'

In June 1908 there was again a special starring engagement at the Alhambra of The Davenports, the Society Entertainers and lightning magicians and illusionists, together with Julia White, comedienne, George White, a descriptive vocalist, The Almas, lightning equilibrists and tumblers, Leon and Noel, vocalists and dancers, Violet Mills, comedienne, and special engagement of Bernard and Weston, the favourite comedians and patterers.

A SPLENDID SOURCE OF AMUSEMENT

Moving on to 1909 and the glowing appreciation of the Theatre's programme is still ongoing. 'The excellent entertainments at the Alhambra are a splendid source of amusement for music hall goers. The management is doing its level best to provide attractive "turns," and this week's programme bears testimony to the success of their efforts. The visit of Takio, the clever Japanese mimic, should prove a great draw. The Jap. who possesses a smile that is most infectious, is a past master in the art of mimicry, and he can imitate realistically anything from a roaring lion to a saxophone One of his must successful imitations is that of a man grinding a knife.'

Taking advantage of the nearby location of the military, the Alhambra in June 1909, promoted wrestling competitions. The publicity for these competitions informed readers that 'There it little doubt that the Alhambra will be packed with an enthusiastic audience to-night (Friday), when the semi-finals for the garrison championship of Shorncliffe Camp as regards wrestling will be decided. Three handsome prizes are aimed; a silver cup stand and two hall-marked silver medals in cases. The competitions are the outcome of a visit to Sandgate of Peter Gots, the well known light ingot wrestler.' During the week Peter Gots had given demonstrations in the of art self-defence and each night he had met military wrestlers who were anxious to qualify for the semi-finals of the competition specially arranged for them.

Then, in the spring of 1910, the Alhambra Theatre was once again temporarily closed for alterations and re-decoration. During the interim, the interior of the hall underwent a thorough renovation to become one of the most comfortable and up-to-date variety theatres in the district. Now lighted throughout by electricity and tastefully painted and decorated, the hall presented a bright appearance. Tip-up red upholstered seats enabled the audience to watch performances in perfect comfort.

However its scheduled re-opening had to be delayed for a short while due to the death of the King. It then finally opened on Monday 23rd May 1910, with a first class international company, including dancing girls from all the principal London and provincial halls.

The opening performances included a lady ventriloquist – something of a novelty – and according to the *Folkestone Express, Sandgate, Shorncliffe & Hythe Advertiser* of the 1st June, 1910, 'the appearance of Miss Florence Raymond was awaited with a certain amount of curiosity. Miss Raymond adopts the role of a nurse and she soon gained the esteem of the critics. It is no easy thing to work the "dolls", but Miss Raymond achieved this difficult performance with enviable ease. The dialogue is very amusing, and Miss Raymond was loudly encored.

PERMISSION FOR CINEMATOGRAPHIC SHOWS

In 1911, the Alhambra applied for a licence to perform stage plays, which was granted, as well as an application for permission to use the premises for cinematographic shows, which was also granted after it was explained that the cinematographic enclosure was outside the building. The Theatre then announced that it had also become an electric theatre, with the newest films being shown every evening by Edward's Imperial Bioscope. It was noted that for Folkestone patrons special cars would leave the Alhambra every evening after the performance, which closes at 10.45.

Charles Kay, with the regular songs, skits and sketch performances that he performed around Kent's coastal resorts gave another of his regular evenings at the Alhambra, Sandgate, in April 1912. The *Folkestone Express, Sandgate, Shorncliffe & Hythe Advertiser* of Saturday 6 April 1912, noted that 'Charles Kay, comedian, is no stranger to the Alhamra, and he was given a reception on Monday night such as is only accorded to established favourites. Charles now appears before the footlights in his Skit entitled 'The Vicar,' the story of a guileless vicar. His success in this role quite puts all previous ones in the shade.'

Just over a year later the *Folkestone Express, Sandgate, Shorncliffe & Hythe Advertiser* of Saturday 26th July, 1913, reported that 'This splendidly fitted music hall is immensely popular, and this week there have been large houses to witness the production of that great drama, "The Price She Paid," by Fox and Henry's London Company. It was a stirring prison drama of a woman who took the place of a man, a murderer. She was sentenced to death. and the prison scenes and the procession to the scaffold were intensely exciting. The escape and confession at the last moment, though, brought a happy ending to the play The play was in four acts. and the scenery was based in the prison at Launceston.'

In May 1914, the licence for stage plays and cinematograph

exhibitions at the Alhambra Theatre of Varieties, Sandgate, was renewed on the application of Mr. Norman Matthews. The Alhambra had continued, under various proprietors over the years, until it was closed in June 1914 following a fire and a period of declining audiences, making it financially unviable. The premises were later put up for auction.

In October 1916, it was announced that the Alhambra had been taken over by the Canadian YMCA as a home-from-home for Canadian soldiers. 'The entrance hall makes a cosy special room where there is always a bright fire burning, and where contemporary literature may be read in comfort. All the private bars have been 'wiped out' and turned into a fine canteen, where refreshments may be obtained by the soldiers at the lowest possible prices. The large music hall, with its stage and gallery boxes will be used for entertainments from time to time, not forgetting the Cinema which is the gift of the Canadian Pacific Railway.'

The Alhambra premises were at various times to become the Sandgate Picture House (June 1921) and then the Rex Cinema in 1939, running as a picture house until June 1951, and later the Rayner's Beach Club. The building was later demolished around 1970 and is now occupied by the Tower Court block of flats.

Looking back over the history of the Alhambra Theatre of Varieties it was noted that 'Sandgate is more favoured than most towns of its size in the matter of entertainment. Of course its proximity to Folkestone, with all its gaieties, enables the residents to share with its bigger neighbour the advantages of Folkestone, but in Folkestone there is no variety theatre pure and simple, so in consequence a good many, especially from the nearby Shorncliffe Garrison, run down to Sandgate for the pleasure of spending the evening in the company of the variety artistes engaged there.

The Sandgate Alhabra is not a place of great proportions but is an extremely comfortable theatre, well lighted by electricity and gas, with orchestra stall, pit stalls, pit dress circle, and boxes. And it has this advantage, that whenever one sits there is a clear and un-interrupted view of the stage, and can hear everything that is said and sung on it. It has undergone many changes during the past thirty years. It is always well patronised. The management has a better class of patrons, and therefore is very careful in its catering.

'To begin with, there is an admirable orchestra. And inasmuch as the vocalists include several of the most fastidious performers seen at the London halls, they insist on the accompanists being well up to the mark. It is quite the usual thing to find in the programme the name of artistes who are doing turns at the London Alhambra, the Palace Theatre, the Coliseum, and the Palladium. It does them good to have a tour of the provincial halls.'

This is perhaps the most fitting epitaph that the Alhambra Theatre of Varieties can have in its memory.

FASHIONABLE FOLKESTONE PIER THEATRE ATTRACTS STAR PERFORMERS

With a successful and quite luxurious music hall/variety theatre almost on its doorstep in Sandgate, it was perhaps not surprising that Folkestone might want to build a bigger and better attraction in the town. From this came a proposal in the early 1880s to form the Folkestone Pier & Lift Company and build an 800 foot long pier, together with a spacious Pavilion at the head of the pier that would have a projected 700 seat capacity, and with additional space for promenading that could accommodate another 1,500, plus potential seating for more people on the promenade roof during regattas. Money raised for the construction would come from the sale of 4,000 shares at £10 each.

Construction of the Victoria Promenade Pier (in honour of the Queen Victoria's 1887 Golden Jubilee) and Pavilion commenced in 1886, with the foundation stone being laid by Viscountess Folkestone

Folkestone's Victoria Promenade Pier and Pavilion Theatre

on the 7th May, 1887. Many thousands of people viewed the stone laying proceedings from the Lees and as near as they could get to the ceremony. Flags and bannerets were said to be flying in all directions. Over the stone there was placed a shield bearing the arms of the Pleydell-Bouverie family. The mayor of Folkestone and people connected with public companies in Folkestone were also present.

The finished length of the pier ended up at just under 700 feet (not the proposed 800 feet) and its width 31 feet; the whole structure being supported by iron piles. At the head of the pier was a spacious 100 foot long and 60 foot wide pavilion which was said to be admirably suited for dances, concerts, theatrical and variety performances, or other entertainments. Such performances on a promenade pier were expected to be a novelty for both Folkestone's inhabitants and for visitors to the town.

The pavilion was provided with a smoking gallery at the back, together with additional space for club, cloakroom and refreshment facilities. A stage was constructed at the north end of the pavilion and was claimed to secure every comfort to both the audience and performers. The total cost of the finished pier and pavilion, plus provision for working capital was at £31,750.

The report on the stone laying ceremony that appeared in the *Folkestone Chronicle* of Saturday 14th May 1887, commented that 'During the stone laying ceremony the consulting engineer for the pier construction, Mr William Wilson, said he believed that the pier would be a great ornament to the town, and afford pleasure to the inhabitants, and to visitors who will be drawn in greater numbers than ever before to this favourable resort.'

The new Victoria Promenade Pier was ideally constructed in one of most convenient parts of the Folkestone coastline, being situated immediately opposite to the Lift, which carried people up the charming slope to the Lees, or brings them down, for the nominal fee of one penny. It was said that as many as 5,000 people had actually paid the one penny toll in a single day.

The Victoria Pier and Pavilion was due to be officially opened by Viscountess Folkestone – who had laid the foundation stone – at 3 o'clock on the afternoon of July 21st, 1888. According to a report of the opening day in the *Folkestone Chronicle* of the same date, 'Those on the spot could hardly believe that the morning's chaos could be transformed into anything like order by the three o'clock opening time. The spacious and handsome pavilion at the seaward end of the Pier looked as if had just appeared as if in a volcanic eruption. The chairs were there, but apparently in a state of hopeless confusion. The stage for the orchestra was topsy-turvey. The refreshment department appeared equally unready. At noon a gas stove had only just been placed in position, and pots , plates and glasses were apparently in confusion.'

At the shore end of the Pier the confusion on the opening day was said to be even worse, yet beautiful patterns of blooming plants and trim paths all seemed to magically appear by late morning and early afternoon, while flags of all nations on masts were shaking in the brisk westerly wind. By the evening Chinese lanterns and fairy lights were being suspended for due effect.

All the necessary work however, was all done in time for the opening and refreshments, drinks and cigars were forthcoming for the invited guests. By the three o'clock opening time quite a thousand people had assembled in the Pavilion to await the arrival of Lady Folkestone, the Mayor and Mayoress, and members of the Town Council. On her arrival a salute from a miniature cannon was fired; the officials all being radiant in new uniforms, gorgeous with gold lace.

Following the stone laying ceremony and a performance by the Band of the Leinster Regiment, the Viscountess and invited dignitaries partook of refreshments before returning to the hall for a short time to listen to a capital concert programme that included singers, the Pier Choral Society, and the Cremona Band. Miss Sherrington sang "God save the Queen" to close the concert.

All along the top of the Leas was a line of spectators which ranged from one end to the other. Several thousand people were said to have populated the Pier during the afternoon and evening, by which time over 1000 Chinese lanterns and fairy lights had been suspended for due effect. A grand display of fireworks also took place in the evening.

It was generally felt that if the opening day could be taken as an augury of success, then the Pier had a brilliant future. This seemed to be borne out in the following weeks after the opening when, in just one day in August, over 3,000 people alone paid for admission to the Victoria Pier on Monday 13th August. The following week, the number of persons who passed the turnstile's on Saturday by payment or by ticket was over 5000. On Sunday there were upwards of 3000, a great attraction being the sacred concert in the evening. On the next Monday there were 2000 people and on Tuesday upwards of 2,510, That's quite a success story

LARGE AUDIENCES ATTRACTED

The following months of 1888 also showed consistently favourable newspaper reports of the entertainment being presented at the Victoria Pier Pavilion. A report in the *Folkestone Express, Sandgate, Shorncliffe & Hythe Advertiser* of Saturday 29th September said 'The entertainments at the Victoria Pier Pavilion continue to attract large audiences every evening, the weather being particularly favourable for promenading there. The clever Johnson troupe are paying a second visit, and also the Brothers Avones, French clowns.' The Switchback Railway, the "permanent way," is brilliantly lighted, is well patronised, and the lift continues to carry its thousands of passengers.

Also in September 1888, Mr. Mowll appeared before the magistrates on behalf of what he termed the "last and greatest of Folkestone successes" – the Victoria Pier – to give notice of an intended application for a dramatic license for the Pier Pavilion. In December, following the granting of the licence, it was said that 'the class of entertainment at the Victoria Pier had taken a superior turn. During the week a powerful London Company had been drawing capital houses with the popular musical comedy "My Sweetheart."

In 1890, two years after the opening of the pier and pavilion, a floating landing stage was added to the end off the pier head. Unfortunately, this failed to attract any steamer landings and ended up being taken out of service in 1892. This failure, and the high operating costs of the pier, lead to the Folkestone Pier & Lift Company running into financial difficulties, subsequently eased by reforming the Company and taking out a long mortgage.

FOLKESTONE PROMENADE
PIER THEATRE.

Under the direction of the Victoria Pier and Lift
Company.

Manager of the Theatre · · Edward Dale.

SPECIAL

Re-opening Week

Of Dramatic Season, under the immediate direction
of the Pier Company, for the performance of high-
class Drama, Comedy, and Burlesque.

Important Engagement for the Opening Night,

MONDAY, MARCH 7TH,

Of the pleasing and popular London actress,

MISS ALICE RAYNOR.

And her Repertoire Company, including

MR. W. HOWELL POOLE.

MONDAY, TUESDAY, AND FRIDAY,
March 5th, 9th, and 12th,

Will be presented the highly successful Drama by
By Mr. W. Howell Poole, entitled—

**Wronged, or through
the Furnace.**

MONDAY, THURSDAY, and SATURDAY
March 10th, 11th, and 13th,

The Celebrated Drama,

Barnes of New York.

Reserved Seats, 3s. and 2s. Unreserved and Gallery,
1s. Back Seats, 6d.

Children half-price to first, second, and third seats
only.

Tickets at Tolputt's Music Warehouse Booking
Office, Sandgate-road, and at the Theatre, where
plans may be seen and seats secured in advance.
Tickets also to be obtained at the Lees entrance to
the Lift.

Doors Open at 7.30. Commence at 8.

Carriages at 10.30 p.m.

*Advertisement in the Folkestone
Chronicle and Advertiser. March 5th,
1892. Newspaper image © The British
Library Board. All rights reserved.
With thanks to
The British Newspaper Archive
(www.britishnewspaperarchive.co.uk)*

Re-opened by the reformed company as the Folkestone Promenade Pier Theatre in March 1892, a special re-opening for a new Dramatic Season variety programme was presented for the performance, with high-class drama, comedy and burlesque.

The Company continued presenting variety programmes, drama and concerts until, in 1894, the Company took the decision to lease out the pier theatre pavilion, initially to the Keith Prowse entertainment agency for two years, and then to King & Co. for the period 1896 to 1902.

This pier leasing initiative proved to be more successful; local newspaper reports and reviews were quite positive and, by providing well patronized Sunday afternoon variety concerts and enticing stars such a Marie Lloyd to the Pavilion (in 1898), the Folkestone Pier and Lift Company were actually able to make a small profit in some years – although this was never enough to pay a dividend to the shareholders.

A report in the *Folkestone, Hythe, Sandgate & Cheriton Herald* of Saturday 6th August, 1898, perhaps highlights the growing success at the Victoria Pier Pavilion Theatre. It wrote 'Immense audiences have gathered here during the week to enjoy the liberal programmes provided by the enterprising management. The usual Sunday afternoon concerts were again well patronised, and the Herr Moritz Wurm's Blue Viennese Band again charmed all lovers of the real and good in music. Miss Alice Lovenez, the vocalist, met with a flattering reception, and this she richly deserves, for she sings with much discrimination and in excellent taste.

'The morning instrumental concerts, under the cool shade of the awning, appear to increase in popularity, judging by the crowded audiences that assemble daily to enjoy the combined pleasures of music and fresh sea breezes. In regard to the variety entertainment, we have nothing to give but genuine praise. First and foremost is the always delightful band which appears if possible to be growing in still greater favour, and then we have our old favourite Mr. Gurney Russell, with a budget of entirely new songs—and out and outers they are too.'

On the same programme were a clever and original ventriloquist, and a presentation of animated photographs. The following week the programme included the Tiller Troupe of eight dancing girls, Professor Ernest, the human orchestra, and Eddie Ross, serio and dancer, while on the Wednesday evening there would be a grand Confetti Fancy Dress Carnival with music by the 3rd Hussars band. On the August Bank Holiday the programme's principal feature was the ever-popular black-faced entertainers, the Moore and Burgess Minstrels.

The throwing of confetti at the fancy dress carnival was raised when the licence came up for renewal. However, there had been no official complaints made to the Council or the police about the selling and throwing of confetti on the Pier. Indeed, ten time more confetti was sold and thrown outside the Pier gates than on it. The Confetti Carnivals also raised money for charity. The licence renewal was therefore granted.

POPULARITY OF SUNDAY CONCERTS

Following the end of the four-year lease of the Pier Pavilion to King & Co, the Pier Company now leased out the pavilion and, this time, the pier as well, to the Keith Prowse agency for a fee of £7,000, together with a percentage of the gate receipts. This seemed to be a successful arrangement with the *Folkestone Express, Sandgate, Shorncliffe & Hythe Advertiser* of 19th August, 1903, reporting that 'The excellent programmes by Messrs. Keith Prowse and Co., at the Victoria Pier are attracting large numbers of people in the afternoon and evening, with the

Advertisement in The Folkestone Chronicle and Advertiser. Saturday March 5th, 1892. Newspaper image © The British Library Board. All rights reserved. With thanks to The British Newspaper Archive (www.britishnewspaperarchive.co.uk)

Sunday concerts in particular proving very popular.'

A year later, on August 11th, 1904, afternoon and evening special concerts were given to a full house by Harry Randall, the eminent comedian, who received an enthusiastic reception. The famous artiste was said to be in fine form and his repertoire well chosen. His first song, "Not a bad sort, Now, Am I?" created roars of laughter.

Just the previous month, on 13th July, 1904, the celebrated comedian and London's favourite

Arthur Roberts, comedian, appeared at the Victoria Pier in August 1904

comic, Dan Leno, had given a selection from his repertoire at two concerts at the Pier Pavilion. Particularly successful was his song "Am I the landlord, or am I not?" that fairly brought down the house. During his second appearance, he related in droll fashion his experiences attending a day at the races.

Another of the country's leading comedians opened a two day engagement at the Victoria Pier Pavilion on Monday the 5th and then Tuesday 6th August, 1904, when crowds of people witnessed the entertainment provided by Arthur Roberts, comedian, music hall entertainer and actor, and his London Company. His amusing songs included "Topsy-Turvey" and "The Magic of the Eye," both of which were vociferously applauded. He was also well known for his hit song "Daddy Wouldn't Buy Me a Bow Wow," as well as something of a reputation for performing risqué songs. The Pavilion, not surprisingly, was crowded for his performances.

In August 1906 the Pavilion at the Victoria Pier was filled to its utmost capacity for the flying visit of Miss Madge Lessing, the famous London Comedienne, stage actress, singer, pantomime principal boy and celebrated postcard beauty. Teamed with Miss Evie Green, their performances of songs and recitations were thoroughly enjoyed and received a very warm reception. Madge Lessing was to go on to make a number of early film appearances.

*Miss Madge Lessing,
at the Pavilion in 1906*

Harry Randall, said to be a particularly great attraction a the Pier Pavilion, made a re-appearance at the Pavilion in 1906, as did the great Lillie Langtry.

Although Keith Prowse & Company had presented some of the country's leading entertainers at the Pier Pavilion over the previous four years, it was local businessmen Robert and Lloyd Forsyth, leading an entirely new local syndicate, who were to take on the lease in 1907. They largely abandoned the expensive entertainers favoured by Keith Prowse to provide attractions that would be more profitable, such as beauty and baby shows, wrestling competitions, pyrotechnic displays, and cinema.

The Pier opened under the new management in May, 1907, and was soon receiving excellent reviews. The *Folkestone, Hythe, Sandgate & Cheriton Herald* of 31st August reported that 'Never has the Victoria Pier been more popular than it is at present. Success attends every performance. The audiences are always large and enthusiastic, and the programmes presented at each entertainment are of very high order.'

The report went on to say 'For this week the management has secured the services of some notable entertainers. One of the foremost of these is Mendel, the blind Paderewski, who undoubtedly causes quite a sensation by his wonderful mastery of the piano. It seems incredible that a blind man should not only be able to play the instrument splendidly by memory, but that he should, after once hearing any melody played over to him by any member of the audience, be able to repeat it.'

Over the coming months, entertainment at the Pier Pavilion included artistes such as The Dagonets, the London Society Entertainers, who appeared in selections from Gilbert and Sullivan's Operas, including "The Mikado." Other performances came from Rosabel Ladies Orchestra, Li Chang Hi, the famous Chinese conjuror, Volcano, the Herculean sensational athlete, The Jamaica Choir, and

73

Miss Minnie Letta's Sporting Girls. The principal of this athletic troupe is the champion lady pedestrian in the world, who had made a record walk from London to Brighton in eight hours forty minutes. A revolving stage enabled all the Sporting Girls to walk and challenge the audience to come and 'track the track.'

Then in September, 1907, the Victoria Pier hosted a night of nights – a beauty show for men. Over 50 men entered the competition, ranging from clean-shaven men, men with moustaches, dark men, fair men, and men of indescribable colour, including a Frenchman, a Swiss, a Japanese, a Hungarian, a Turk and even a negro. Each contestant came forward and had to push their head through a slit in a black velvet drape suspended in a large gilded frame. The effect was said to be most comical. Judging in the packed hall was by a ballot of the audience, with the winner receiving a Raleigh bicycle and the runner up a silver watch.

In October, 1907, the management announced that the Pier would be entirely renovated inside and out during the winter closed season, with better seating accommodation and improved scenery. The Pier Pavilion would then be re-opened at Easter 1908 and continue right through to the end of September without a break. During the winter the Pavilion was to be cleared for the purpose of turning the place into a skating rink.

Acts appearing in the new season's programme commencing 4th May, 1908, showcased "Pruno's Unrideable and Educated Donkey." The following year a flying visit by the famous Miss Kitty Loftus drew large numbers for a Sunday Concert in two performances. She was said to be enthusiastically recalled and met with hearty applause.

A CHANGE TO ANIMATED PICTURE SHOWS

The management of the Victoria Pier Pavilion opened their 1910 season on May 12th. However, instead of the usual variety show there was an animated picture entertainment in the up-to-date Electric Picture Theatre, said to be one of the safest places of amusement on the Kent coast. The innovation was well attended, and now set the scene for the future of the Pavilion, together with Sunday concerts, open-air skating, and some variety entertainments.

There were still some wonderous turns in the Pavilion over the coming years, including, in August 1913, by "Billy," the horse with a human brain, presented by M. E. Hayes. This wonderful animal could work arithmetical sums, whilst it also made an excellent partner at whist. A couple of weeks later it was possible to see Buckingham's Performing dogs and Hybrid Wolf.

From 1915, the showing of films in the Electric Picture Theatre included many dramas and documentary type films about the War, as well as Charlie Chaplin films, films of boxing matches and sporting events. The showing of films in the Theatre started to decline during the 1920s, compensated by a steady rise in jazz bands.

The condition of the Pier eventually started to decline as the iron piles and wooden decking became corroded and rotten. The Pier was closed at the outbreak of World War ii and then, a few months later the centre portion of the pier was blown up as a defence measure. Then, in May 1945, the sea end of the pavilion structure was destroyed by fire, said to be one of the biggest blazes seen in Folkestone. The last remaining section of the pier was finally blown up in November 1954, so ending some 66 years of concert, variety theatre, cinematic, pyrotechnic and outdoor performance history.

FOLKESTONE'S PLEASURE GARDEN HOME FOR PANTOMIME, LIVE THEATRE AND OPERA

At much the same time as the Victoria Pier and Pavilion were being built in Folkestone for the presentation of dances, concerts, theatrical and variety performances and other entertainments, so another building was being also being constructed in the town as, initially, an exhibition venue and grounds for the Art Treasures Exhibition at a cost of £16,000.

Two years later, in 1888, this exhibition building – with a glass roof similar to the Crystal Palace in London – was purchased and taken over by the newly formed Folkestone Pleasure Gardens Company, with the promoters' aiming to convert the building and grounds into a place of general entertainment that would be very advantageous to the town. They also anticipated making a profit and to be able to pay a good dividend to shareholders. The converted building was renamed as the Exhibition Palace Theatre, with the capability of accommodating upwards of twelve hundred people, significantly more than the Victoria Pier Pavilion.

The first entertainment in the new Theatre was a pantomime. Attended by Lord and Lady Folkestone and an aristocratic party, as well as a large number of the principal inhabitants of the town's west end; attendance was said to be much larger than it would have been if still held in the Town Hall. It fully realized the expectations of the promoters as potentially a great source of attraction in Folkestone, both during the summer and winter.

The results of the early entertainments given in the Exhibition Palace Theatre were certainly most encouraging for the syndicate

Folkestone Pleasure Gardens Theatre

who had purchased the building and adapted it as a place of general entertainment. The lighting of the transept had been most successfully accomplished and the gas lighting was preferred to the cold lighting obtained by means of appliances. The attendance at the opening pantomime were much larger than it would have bean able to accommodate in the Town Hall. On just one day of the pantomime for instance, there were upwards of twelve hundred people admitted. Lord and Lady Folkestone and an aristocratic party, together with a large number of the principal inhabitants of the west end were present.

The *Folkestone Chronicle* of Saturday 14th January, 1888, commented that 'There is every prospect that as a place of entertainment it will fully realize the expectations of the promoters and not only be a great source of attraction to the town, both in summer and winter, but that judiciously worked will pay a dividend on the very moderate capital which will be necessary to carry it on.'

By the September of 1888, the Theatre was still drawing large audiences, this time to see Mr. Thomas Thorne's Vaudeville Company who were visiting the theatre on the Friday and Saturday with "Joseph's Sweetheart." The following month the Pleasure Gardens Theatre discontinued concerts and entertainments for a short period for certain structural alterations and additions to the building.

Local comment in 1892 was that, 'either by accident or design, the principal places of amusement in Folkestone, namely the Pleasure Gardens Theatre and the Victoria Pier Theatre, seldom clashed in their presentations because, as a rule, the entertainments were as widely different as it was possible to be.'

FOLKESTONE PLEASURE GARDENS THEATRE

Programmes of general and variety entertainment, as well as annual pantomimes at the Theatre, continued to be well attended over the coming few years until, in April 1896, it was again remodelled and now renamed as the Pleasure Gardens Theatre. It's opening production was of "A Trip to Chicago," staged by Walter Sealby's Company.

Just a few months later, In June 1896, the Theatre became the first venue in Kent to screen moving pictures. In 1913, the foyer was enlarged, now enabling it to be additionally used as a concert hall. The Pleasure Gardens Theatre now became home to drama presentations, pantomimes, opera performances and touring productions from London's leading theatres.

Pantomimes were to be a key Christmas entertainment at the Theatre over the years. These were usually touring productions that would spend two weeks at each theatre, Folkestone's turn usually being in the first couple of weeks of each January. Said to be three hours full of fun and free from vulgarity, the Christmas 1900 pantomime was "Puss in Boots" which, from first to last had a genuine swing about the production, in which there was not a single 'blue' line.

Immediately prior to the Puss in Boots pantomime, in late December 1900, the famous London comedian, Arthur Roberts, commenced his own engagement at the Theatre.

The following year, in January 1902, the delightful pantomime presented was "Beauty and the Beast" which boasted of exquisite Scenery, Superb Costumes, Charming effects and Enchanting Music. The entire pantomime company and production came directly from the Royal County Theatre, Kingston-on-Thames. The January 1903 pantomime was "The Sleeping Beauty". In January 1904 the grand pantomime was "Cinderella."

During each year the Pleasure Gardens Theatre would present dramatic theatre, opera and musical performances given by leading London and national touring groups, including regular visits during the 1900s by Shakespeare touring companies, presenting "Romeo and Juliet," "Twelfth NIght," "The Taming of the Shrew," "As you like it," as well as visits from the D'Oyly Carte repertoire Opera Company to present "The Mikado" or the W. S. Gilbert Opera Co., to present "The Daughter of the Regiment."

In May 1906 there was whole week of Shakespeare, Hamlet and Macbeth, while a "Hamlet" production at the Theatre in February 1908, which the *Folkestone, Hythe, Sandgate & Cheriton Herald* of

Saturday 22nd February, 1908, noted there was 'Great interest and a large audience for "Hamlet". A magnificent production in which the moody Dane of Mr. Irving was a profound study brilliant executed with a rare elocutionary skill, and the mounting of the tragedy was on a fine scale.

1908 seemed to be a notable year for other distinguished performances. In June of that year the Theatre was host to Madame Sarah Bernhardt and her distinguished company direct from the Theatre Sarah Bernhardt, Paris, in "La Dame aux Camelias" by Alexander Duma. Although born in Paris in 1844, she made her name on stages throughout Europe and America from the 1870s, as well as having a sporadic love affair with early cinema.

This was followed in July by Mr. Fred Karno's Company appearing at

Dame Sarah Bernhardt in "La Dame aux Camelias"

Fred Karno and his Company appeared at the Pleasure Gardens in July 1908

the Theatre performing "His Majesty's Guests," a production which was described a musical pantomimical farce. There was said to be some semblance of a plot, with the main point being that a couple of thieves, styling themselves as Lord Easem and Lady Maud Easem were raiding the country house and London emporium of Mr. Milin, with Sergeant Lightning, a caricature of a policeman, endeavouring to catch the marauders.

The Pleasure Gardens Theatre was also used for amateur and charitable performances. In December 1910, members of the Folkestone Dramatic Club occupied the Theatre for three nights, performing "Beauty and the Barge," a comedy, in aid of the Poor Children's Fund. Large audiences resulted in a substantial amount being handed over to the Charity Committee.

Excellent dramatic performances were the order throughout the period between 1910 and 1920. Too many to highlight in these pages, although for those that are interested it is possible to find a great deal of further information in the archives of the British Newspaper Archive. Nevertheless, it might be worth picking out a few of the more interesting or dramatic performances over the years.

Lusty demonstrations of approval and delight, especially from the pit and the gallery, were forthcoming in July 1912 when Mr. Travis Green's Company opened a week's engagement in the Red Indian Romantic play, "Queen of the Redskins." The play was said to illustrate the racial distinction between the whites and the redskins. The queen in the play being Wahneetah, who is loved by Bronco Bill.

Large audiences were also attracted to the Theatre when "The Follies" presented a highly diverting entertainment in June 1914. The entertainment was said to be excellent throughout, with the burlesque of a music hall keeping the 'houses' in a high state of merriment.

Sunday concerts were to play an important part in the Theatre's annual programmes of events, with perhaps few being more prestigious than the Grand Concert presented by Madame Clara Butt on Sunday 14th January 1917. One of the country's most popular singers in the late 1800s and first twenty years of the 1900s, Clara Butt had an exceptionally fine contralto voice, with composers, such as Elgar, composing songs with her in mind. She was later made a Dame (in 1920)

Miss Clara Butt presented a Grand Concert at The Pleasure Gardens Theatre in January 1917

The Theatre continued to draw some of the best dramatic plays, singers, actors and actresses. In October 1918, it was the turn of Miss Jane Wood, said to be one of the greatest emotional actresses ever seen on any stage, and in Folkestone, playing the part of a prostitute who becomes a music hall entertainer and the mistress of a married man in "Zaza," a play originally written in French. The *Folkestone, Hythe, Sandgate & Cheriton Herald* highlighted 'Her overwhelming passion, with its lightning transition to laughing, love making and most tenderly beseeching moments are quite natural.'

In what was described as the biggest West-End Cast ever toured, the 1919 Whitsuntide attraction at The Pleasure Gardens Theatre was the musical comedy "His Little Widows," in which every line is a roar of laughter and every song a lasting winner. The cast included Marie Blanche, a musical comedy actress and late leading lady from the Drury Lane pantomime. At the time of her appearance in Folkestone she was also staring in a film produced by the Stoll Film Company entitled "The Exclusive Pimpernel."

Although revues were rare productions at the Theatre in the 1920s, in August 1923, the town was privileged to have a visit from "Pot Luck," the revue in which Jack Hulbert and Cicely Courtneidge had carried London by storm. The revue presented was exactly the same as that in London, with the two of them, and their merry and clever assistants, won the highest accolades at every performance. Cicely Courtneidge later became a Dame.

Known as the "British King of Jazz" and the "Ambassador of British Dance Music," Jack Hylton, the famous English pianist, composer, jazz and band leader, gave two Sunday concerts at the

Jack Hylton and his Orchestra drew crowded house at the Pleasure Gardens Theatre on Good Friday 1835

Theatre on the 17th June 1928. Indeed, he gave over 40 concerts in Folkestone over the years. However, it was another ten years before he appeared at the Pleasure Gardens Theatre again, on Easter Sunday 1935. Billy Cotton and his Band drew crowded houses when they paid their first visit to the Theatre on the previous Good Friday 1935.

Famous entertainers continued to be attracted to the Pleasure Gardens Theatre well into the 1920s. August 1927 saw the famous music hall entertainer and male impersonator, Ella Shields and her party at the Theatre for three nights on Sunday, August 21st. Although born in America, she achieved her greatest success in England and was especially noted for her famous signature song, "Burlington Bertie from Bow," which was written for her by her first husband and manager, William Hargreaves

Then in December 1928, it was the turn of The Great Cosmo, the famous illusionist, who was the vaudeville attraction for the

A caricature of Ella Shields performing as Burlington Bertie

week commencing December 17th, while Paul Robeson, the wonderful singer came to the Pleasure Gardens Theatre for a return Sunday concert visit on the 3rd August, 1929, where he gave a special programme of Negro music.

This was later followed by a great celebrity Sunday concert event on February 23rd 1930 when Kubelik the world-renowned master violinist gave his only UK appearance after returning from his tenth World Tour. It was during this year that Walter Bentley took over the running of the Theatre.

Pantomime's were still a key part of the Theatre's promotions even into the 1930s. January 1930, saw the management present their 23rd gorgeous Xmas Pantomime; an entirely new Murray King version of "Cinderella." In 1935 it was "Jack and the Beanstalk."

In August 1935, Elsie and Doris Waters came to the Theatre to relive the days of big audiences and great stars of the vaudeville stage, contributing to an entertainment that was said to be faultless and extensive in its appeal, with the box office breaking records.

Just a few months later the Union Cinema chain took over the management of the Theatre. Although a cinema chain, they still continued presenting live theatre shows.

The Theatre closed for a while in 1956 to enable structural alterations to take place, including the removal of pillars and the lowering of the ceiling in the foyer/concert. It was then fitted out with the latest film projection equipment and opened as a cinema only. This did not prove to be a great success. The cost of running a 1500 seat capacity cinema and, with the building becoming rundown and needing urgent renovation, it was finally closed down in May 1964.

The building was converted into a bingo club. Lasting only a short time it ended up being demolished. Today, an office block and large car park occupy the site, which is now used by the Kent Police.

IMMENSE AND FASHIONABLE AUDIENCE FOR OPENING OF DOVER THEATRE

The Tivoli Theatre in Snargate Street, Dover, opened its doors on Monday 14th June 1897 in the presence of an immense and fashionable audience that were reported in the *Dover Express* as being 'amazed and delighted by a playhouse that for richness of furnishings, beauty of design, comfort and convenience could not be surpassed on the South Coast.' Designed internally by C. J. Phipps, a well-known theatre designer, the stalls, dress circle, pit and the gallery were all perfect examples of what a theatre should be, 'and there was not a single place in the auditorium from which a splendid view of the stage could not be obtained.'

With 500 seats in the stalls, four private boxes, plus the circle and gallery and five bars, it was expected that Dover's residents would soon learn to regularly book, at least once a week, to enjoy the plays and vaudeville acts that were booked to appear at the theatre. Owned by the Dover Tivoli Ltd., a company formed in 1896, and built by Harry Richardson of Dover, the construction cost was put at £15,000.

The day's opening proceedings commenced at eleven o'clock in the morning with an application to the Council for a dramatic and musical licence, which was granted, the Councillors complimenting Mr. Amand Mascard, the theatre manager, upon the enterprise of his directors, and thanking them for the faith they had in the London Press.

In the afternoon a matinee was given primarily for the benefit of the representatives from the London Press, but which was also attended by local townsfolk. The early newcomers to the matinee

89

were particularly interested in seeing the stage set for the "Tea House of Ten Thousand Joys."

The main function of the opening day took place in the evening, when an assembly, headed by the Mayor and Corporation, Sir W. Butler and Officers of the Garrison and their families, and containing the elite of the town, gathered within the Theatre's walls, filling it to repletion. According to the *Dover Chronicle* of the 19th June, 'all bookable seats had been secured by the Saturday night, and many paid for the privilege of standing. The verdict with regard to the building and the class of entertainment produced was not for one moment in doubt. Applause, long, hearty and genuine, signalled the parting of the beautiful crimson plush tableau curtains, and growing in intensity as success after success was achieved, and all terminating in a hurricane of demonstration that was not appeased till the curtain had been twice raised, and Mr. Mascard had come forward and bowed his acknowledgments.'

It was widely stated that a no more happier choice of an opening piece could have been made, or one calculated to impress the audience with the high class of entertainment that the Tivoli Theatre intended to provide, than the fine company of vocalists and light comedians engaged by Mr. Morell and Mouillot to perform 'The Geisha."

'The really splendid all round excellence of the cast, 'reported the *Dover Chronicle*, 'proved possession of rare powers and discriminations, for not a part was miscast, nor could either of the clever performers have been bettered. The play's charming lyrics, and exquisite setting, and the resource of its comedians made amends for any shortcomings, for when not encoring delightfully rendered numbers, the audience is laughing its hardest at expositions of humour whimsically conceived, and drolly designed.'

By early August 1897 the Tivoli Theatre was already breaking new records when the tuneful and humorous musical lady "The Shop Girl" made its bow over the first three nights of the week, followed in the next three days by the phenomenally successful farcical comedy, "A Night Out," said to be one of the most screamingly funny plays ever written.

A report on the week's programmes added that Mr Mascard, always looking to the comfort of his patrons, had installed electric bells in each private box which communicated directly with the buffet so that ices, etc., could be immediately obtained without patrons having to move to seek an attendant. It also added that 'the staircase leading to the dress circle, the grand entrance, and all along the promenade had been adorned with handsome palms placed so as to refresh the eyes and gracefully embellish these parts of the building.'

Regular performances of dramatic and comedic plays continued with success throughout the rest of 1897, interspersed with regular vaudeville, burlesque and variety shows, all leading up to the Tivoli's first pantomime – "Babes in the Wood" – being presented in February and March of 1898. Attracting good audiences, the *Dover Express* of 1st March commented that Mr. Hunter's pantomime 'deserved to be called something better that a pantomime, being far superior to the common run of that description of entertainment, and one that could be enjoyed by any grown person as much as a child.'

At the end of March 1898, the Dover Tivoli Ltd, company held its first annual general meeting to present to shareholders the first report and balance sheet dealing with the affairs of the Company and the theatre, which it said had been built on the site of the old Royal Clarence Theatre, which itself had opened back in 1790 and was demolished in 1897.

The Directors reported that, since the theatre's opening, the business of the Theatre had been conducted to their satisfaction, with results which were most encouraging. The erection of the theatre had been paid for, arrangements for supplying refreshments to the public had been completed, and the Directors were more than satisfied with the profits upon this branch of the business. Since the completion of the bar in Snargate Street, the financial returns had been almost doubled. Electric lighting had now been installed throughout the entire building

In their report the Directors mentioned that about 40 theatrical touring groups in all had visited Dover during its first year, and that the theatre had met with the unqualified approval of all the visiting companies. Nevertheless, the class of entertainments could still be much improved, and could doubtless result in an increase of the receipts. The report also stated that there had been representations to the Directors that some misunderstanding had arisen owing to the present title of the theatre, so, with a view to prevent any misconception as to the class of entertainments, the Directors proposed to change the name of the theatre to the Tivoli Theatre Royal, which title, under the charter, they have a right to assume. This was agreed, and was set to take place at the end of July 1898.

Just one month after the company's AGM the theatre was presenting "Little Red Riding Hood," a smart little burlesque produced by Miss

Violet Gray's Company. Described as a pretty, bright, humorous, and laughable play, closely resembling pantomime, but superior to the ordinary run, it included some really very melodious music, and in addition, plenty of comic songs. The story of the adventures of Red Riding Hood and her meeting with the wolf were told pretty much the same as in the old story, although there were a few adaptations, and there's a Prince Amoroso who rescues the heroine from the monster.

In June 1898 the theatre presented the sensational American musical comedy drama "Down the Slope," followed by the charming musical play "My Sweetheart," which had a chorus of pretty children. The *Dover Chronicle* advertisement for this programme, and for the following advertisements during the year, now carried the message 'Theatre Patrons' Bicycles stored free of charge at the Theatre during the performances.' A further note at

TIVOLI THEATRE, DOVER.
Telephone No. 325.

Proprietors .. .. The Dover Tivoli, Ltd.
Manager .. .. .. Mr. Amand Mascard.

LAST TWO NIGHTS OF
CHAS. F. TINGAY'S
Celebrated Dramatic Company, in the latest Sensational American Musical Comedy Drama,

"DOWN THE SLOPE."

MONDAY, JUNE 20th, for six nights only.
The Charming Musical Play—

"MY SWEETHEART,"

New Songs! New Funny Sayings! New Business!
Everything Up-to-Date. Tuneful, Sparkling, Delightful, Graceful.

CHORUS OF PRETTY CHILDREN.

Amongst the Songs introduced by Mr. Lunn and Miss Sotter will be the following—

"See Saw," Song and Chorus .. Tony and Children
"Over the Hills ".. .. .. .. Tony
"I'm so Shy," Song and Dance .. .. Tina
"The Cuckoo Duet" .. .. Tony and Tina
"They Say" .. .. Tina
"Coaxing Duet" .. .. .. Tony and Tina
"Medley Duet" .. .. .. Tony and Tina
"Tina, Forgive Me" .. .. Tony and Tina
"Drink Boys" .. .. Tony
And the ever-popular "Peek-a-Boo" .. .. Tony
Musical Director (For "My Sweetheart" Co.)
Mr. J. H. Yorke.

N.B.—Theatre Patrons' Cycles Stored Free of Cost at the Theatre during the Performances.

Doors Open at 7.15. Commence at 7.45.
Prices of Admission—Private Boxes, £1 1s. 0d. and £1 11s. 6d.; Dress Circle, 3s.; Stalls, Reserved 2s. 6d., and 2s. at Theatre Door; Pit, 1s.; Gallery, 6d.

Early Doors at 7.0 to all parts 6d. extra.
Bonnets not allowed in first two Rows of Dress Circle.

Box-Office now open at the Theatre from 11 till 4.

The Dover and County Chronicle,
Saturday June 18th, 1898. Newspaper
image © The British Library Board. All
rights reserved. With thanks to
The British Newspaper Archive
(www.britishnewspaperarchive.co.uk).

the bottom of the advertisement stated that 'Bonnets not allowed in front two rows of the Dress Circle.'

Another musical play or comic opera followed in July 1898 when "The Skirt Dancer" appeared at the theatre. The *Dover Express* of Friday 15th July reported that 'On visiting the Tivoli on Monday it was easily seen that this new work would be a success, for right away from the opening chorus there was plenty of swing and go, but not of a pace that was too fast to last.' It went on to comment that 'The most welcome feature about the performance was the absence of that boring nuisance achieved by flopping about the stage in a manner that a duck waddles and shakes its wings, which is termed skirt dancing. Instead of this, which the silly posters led a good many to expect, there was a really good show.

Just a couple of weeks later a visit by the Moore and Burgess Minstrels to the Tivoli provided a welcome change of programme, and was quite distinct from anything else the theatre had presented. This was seen as a very good thing for the Tivoli, as Moore and Burgess have a "clientele" of their own. The programme altered each night, so 'there was little advantage in criticising it all beyond expressing general approval.' On the Friday night there was a performance under the patronage of the Mayor and Corporation, during which a new "coon" song was sung by Mr. Leo Moor, with a chorus by the Company.

Following the decision made at the AGM, the management of the theatre announced on the 26th August 1898 that the name of the 'Tivoli" was now being changed to "The Theatre Royal." The change, they explained, had been long been contemplated, and was a very suitable one, conveying a better idea of the entertainment provided, which is usually "right royal fare."

Mr. D'Oyly Carte's repertoire Company visited the Theatre Royal during the same week, and had given some excellent representations of the Savoy masterpieces. On Monday night "The Mikado," the most popular of English comic opera, produced by Mr. C. Wallem, was excellent, with the music on the whole fairly rendered. The songs, and the beautiful madrigal, were enthusiastically encored, and excellently sung. Several of the other popular airs were also called a second time.

The first three nights of the week commencing 14th November 1898, brought a well-received musical extravaganza to the Theatre Royal, entitled "Naughty Mr. Bluebeard," in which the story was told to the accompaniment of songs which caught the attention of the audience. This was followed later in the week by "The Belle of the West," a Wild West play which included some highly sensational scenes, and introducing a number of acting dogs and horses.

In January 1899 "Uncle Tom's Cabin" appeared at the Theatre Royal in a presentation that had some novel interesting features in the fact that the majority of the actors were real negroes. 'This sensational drama,' as reported by the *Dover Express*, 'was acted with moderation and skill, with some staging of plantation hymns in the true darkey style. Uncle Tom was played by a negro without any make-up, and looking his part.'

Just a couple of weeks later, on Friday and Saturday in early February, Mr. Bramston Trent gave an exhibition of his skill in producing magical illusions, as well as giving experiments in

95

thought transference, while Mr. W. J. Hilliar performed some tricks which relied purely on sleight of hand. The entertainment was very successful and deserved a larger audience that that actually present. This was followed on the Monday by the brilliant pantomime "Beauty and the Beast," in which there was plenty of fun. The *Dover Express* of the 10th February reported that 'the best song is "Danger on the line," supposedly sung by a railway porter, with pretty effects obtained with alternating white, red and green lights, which a large and well-balance chorus carry.'

Another pantomime was presented in early March that year, when Mr. Henry Roxbury's grand comic pantomime, "Cinderella," made a welcome reappearance at the Theatre Royal, but with new songs and business now introduced. There were also some clever gymnasts in a very skilfully performed representation that was first class – a term which could be applied to the whole entertainment.

Drama, comedy and farce, interspersed with variety shows, continued to be the a staple at the Theatre Royal during the early 1900s, together with regular annual pantomimes and opera. Although it's not feasible to discuss all of these, it is perhaps interesting to pick out a few programmes of interest.

In June 1903, Miss Nita Rae's company presented "The Lunatics," a farcical musical comedy which created roars of laughter in a tale of topsy-turveydom from start to finish, and the amusing situations caused by the playfulness of a boy, which was reported in the *Dover Chronicle* as being 'excruciatingly funny.' The scene of the piece took place at Brighton, with everybody chasing everybody else round the "Queen's" hotel and Brighton Pier from morn till night, until explanations ensue the following morning.

"Dick Whittington and his Cat" paid a late visit to the Theatre Royal in May 1905 when Miss Lena Stanton's Company presented a well produced pantomime containing smart and witty songs and dialogue, new and beautiful scenery, dances and specialities. The prime favourite was reported as Little Keno, a juvenile prodigy, who was promoted as the Juvenile Dan Leno, who sings, dances, acts, and makes a great deal of fun. Other acts in the pantomime included acrobatic dancers, ventriloquism, and La Belle Esma's performances on the "Silver Thread" which marked her out as an expert in Blondin's art.

Experimenting with a variety show in July 1905 proved such a success that they were then repeated twice nightly, at 7 and 9 o'clock. With numerous first-class turns that included Mddlle. Roseltha, a very smart international and skip-rope dancer, Wragg and Wragg, the military athletes – who performed the very smart feat of cutting the carcase of a sheep in half with one blow – The Rosaires, with their reputation as the greatest living acrobats, and the Franklin Troupe of Russian dancers, who contributed a performance never before seen in Dover.

Moving to May 1906, the Theatre Royal presented at enormous expense, the famous Prima Donna, Madam Emma Nevada. This famous singer delighted everyone, not only by her beautiful voice and wonderful elocution, but by the great expression and magnificent sympathy with which she touched all hearts. She was loudly applauded upon each appearance and for one of her encores she sang "Home Sweet Home," the rendering of which the *Dover Chronicle* noted 'will linger in the memory of those who were privileged to hear her.'

Royal Hippodrome picture courtesy of Paul Skelton, Dover Kent Archives. Pub-info@Dover-Kent.com

With variety and vaudeville proving increasingly popular, the Theatre Royal continued to look for new and entertaining acts that could be presented in Dover. Amongst the performers in March 1907 were Bert Fox, Glenroy and Cross, May Kent and Terris (with his panikins), but now adding in to the programme, Payne's Bio-Photoscope moving pictures, including "The Wreck of the Berlin."

Three months later and the Theatre is now presenting animated pictures at two houses a night for a whole week. The programme at the end of June, by Messrs. Barnett and Tindell's Company, provided an endless variety of films of the very best character. Variety acts are now interspersed with the films. On the variety bill was Little Edie, the child vocalist; Lilie Le Breton, a very smart trapeze artiste; Le Brun and Mdlle. Irene, equilibrists and double jugglers; and Miss Kate Kyrie, who illustrated her songs using a bioscope.

A change of ownership took place in January 1908, as well as a change in the name of the Theatre Royal, both announced in the *Dover Express* of 20th December 1907, which said that Mr. F. C. Drew, the theatre manager would take a bumper farewell benefit and be given a good send-off by his Dover friends. The new Proprietor, Mr. Winter, would be undertaking extensive alterations to the theatre, with the pit re-seated to increase the accommodation, the whole house re-decorated and re-upholstered. It was reported that the refurbished theatre would re-open for performances under the new regime on Monday 3rd February, 1908, and would then be known as the Royal Hippodrome.

At the re-opening night, Mr. Sidney Winter, the new proprietor announced a first class variety programme. This was of a similar kind to the types of music hall and variety performances that he intended to present in the future. At each of the performances during the week, the great riding machine, one of the funniest acts ever seen, would be given at each performance. Silver cups would be given on the Friday night for the boy standing on the pony twice round. Silver cups would also be given for anyone riding the unrideable mule twice round.

A few weeks later, opening on the 16th March, the Royal Hippodrome had a crowded audience for the Turkish Tom Thumb, claimed to be the smallest man in the world, who commenced a week's engagement. The 56 year old entertainer at just 36 inches high, and

Tiny-Town, Olympia Annexe.
The Turkish Tom Thumb. Lost in London.

An early photograph of the Turkish Tom Thumb, the smallest man in the world

weighing 34 pounds, proved a great draw and was a very smart turn. On the bill with him was Langslow, the balancing marvel, who brought the house down with his shooting; Boneti and Corri, eccentric jugglers; Mdlle. Pollo Jerome, a refined lady gymnast; and Miss Eileen Douglas, with her charming songs and dainty dances.

Then in late April/early May the management of the Royal Hippodrome were congratulated upon securing an array of leading variety artistes, such as the one appearing during the week commencing 27th April, when Queenie Leighton, a Drury Lane favourite, rendered in a delightful manner a number of tuneful songs and introducing topical local topics which were enthusiastically received, her great hit being "Just a little bit of parsley." Great enthusiasm prevailed at the conclusion of the number.

Another notable artist on the same bill was Will English, a popular London coloured comedian. Regarded as one of the cleverest comedians to appear in Dover, his songs were of the latest and brimming over with good humour. Apart from his vocal items, he introduced a novelty with "He of the walks," in which he gave an exhibition of different styles of walking, the "Conservative and the Liberal" walk, which was said to exceptionally good. A pantomime sketch entitled "Ye Olde Bow Inn" by Berg, Hand and Wise, created roars of laughter. Hippodrome pictures concluded an excellent evening.

Another capital programme of first-class music hall stars took place at the Royal Hippodrome at he end of December 1908, with every artist being warmly applauded. Richly amusing was Mamie Brent, a low comedy artiste with a sweet voice and chic bearing. Her song "She left the door ajar" caused roars of laughter. She was followed by Nat Travers, the King of Coster Comedians, whose repertoire included genuine coster experiences, including the one about "The driver of a London dust-cart," all his stories being given in full coster character.

Also on the bill were the Two Lillies, vocalists and dancers, who were rapturously applauded for their act which was said to be one of the very best ever seen on the boards at the Hippodrome. Their graceful dancing, in which they successfully duplicate each other, appears as if one person is dancing in front of a mirror. Every items was said to be perfect, and it was not until the second dancer comes forward that the audience realises that any duplication has actually taken place. Their skip-rope dancing was equally delightful. Kate Weston, a comedienne and coon artiste rendered a song in capital fashion and merited enthusiastic recalls.

Charles Pastor, a London character comedian also kept the audience in roars of laughter. His patter as a swell "awfully fond of dancing," was hilariously told, swaggering his story in amusing fashion. His second item as a knowing woman of the alley was equally as great, and his descriptive song as "Mrs. Martin, the 'magger,' " was replete with ridiculous patter in which there was more to be said, if, as she says, "she hadn't got the dinner on the hob." He was warmly recalled.

First-class and, often, unusual variety and vaudeville entertainment acts continued throughout 1909, with performances by artistes that included Elton and Edwin, world champion banjoists; Maud Edmond, the original "Charlie Brown" girl; Queenie May, a delightful child vocalist; Byron, the comedy clay modeller who produced models representing the features of Shakespeare and North American Indians; and Les Hale, fresh from America, as a skate dancer, who gave clever trick dances on a pair of genuine roller skates.

Especially amusing in February 1909 were Hemsley and Ambrose in their original motor car absurdity, "The coster's honeymoon," which opened with a motor car which comes to a standstill when trouble begins. Tyre after tyre burst until all four have gone; then the engine goes wrong and miniature explosions occur. They try to repair by reading the car handbook. They are 50 miles from anywhere. They have a tiff, and she wishes she had gone on honeymoon on the coster's tandem instead. The acts ends when a notice is hoisted saying that the car is for sale.

Another novel performance came from Talberto and Douglas, the "awful acrobats," who presented a laughable turn full of knockabout business and ludicrous situations. Their pedal ball performance was smartly done, and included clever balancing skill. The turn caused continuous laughter to the very end. Equally novel was the performance by Miss. Jennie Hously and Mr. B. Nathan, which was set in the drawing room of a lunatic asylum and was brimful of quaint situations and drolleries of the rarest description.

Unusual among animal acts at the Royal Hippodrome were E. H. Bostock's Baboons, a remarkably clever troupe of animals introduced by Captain Grahame. The manner in which they performed numerous feats and tricks was reported by the *Dover Express* of August 27th, 1909, as very striking, and that they were almost human in their movements. Rather different was Joe Belmont, who styled himself as the "Human Bird," who imitated in a most realistic fashion the songs of different birds, his representation of a canary being the most striking.

The second decade of the 1900s saw the Royal Hippodrome continue with its successful, full houses and widely applauded music hall, burlesque and variety shows, including some of the best UK and International performers, and enhancing the theatre's reputation as the Premier Theatre of Varieties in Dover. George Roger, a funny Frenchman made his first appearance in England at the Dover theatre, giving in broken English his rendition of "Napoleon of the Boulevard," followed by him giving a very funny impersonation of a French headmaster, which created roars of laughter, and as an encore, he gave a Frenchman's idea of a "can-can" in rag-time. Charles Kay, comedian, also once again made an appearance at a Kent seaside theatre.

In January 1923 the Royal Hippodrome presented the pretty musical pantomime, "The Home of the Fairies," an enhancing story of a child's dream of Fairyland in quest of her father, which included many picturesque scenes and enhancing dresses, and some very clever dancing and singing. The *Dover Chronicle* of 6th January 1923 noted that 'Not only is it a first class pantomime for children, but one full of interest for adults.'

Musical comedy revue and sketch companies also regularly, and increasingly, visited the Royal Pavilion during the second and third decades of the 1900s. A great attraction being the appearance in July 1913 of the original Six Brothers Luck, who presented what was said to be the greatest comedy sketch produced in recent years, entitled "H.M.S. Perhaps." This sketch came to Dover following enormous success in London and provincial theatres. The showing of Hippodrome animated and pictures films interspersed with, or following, the variety acts also continued throughout this second and third decades of the 1900s.

Variety programmes at the Royal Hippodrome in the early 1940s included many well-known radio and stage artists such as Sandy Powell, the famous B.B.C. comedian; Albert Whelan; Albert Grant, the Worker's Playtime comedian; Nellie Wallace; Tommy Trinder; Beryl Reid; and Miss. Evelyn Laye, as well as speciality performers like Anna Marita, advertised on the billboard as a speciality dancer and glamorous nude.

The theatre also advertised in The *Dover Express and East Kent News* of 26th April 1940, for a brave girl who would be prepared to be fired from an electric cannon by The Great Levante's. Pantomimes were also still being presented during the 1940s, the Grand Christmas Pantomime "Cinderella," running throughout the week in January 1944.

ROYAL HIPPODROME

WANTED !!
THE BRAVEST GIRL IN DOVER !
To be fired from
THE GREAT LEVANTE'S Electric Cannon
at the Second House — Tuesday Night.
HEIGHT: 5 ft.   WEIGHT: 8 st.
Apply:—THE MANAGER, HIPPODROME, DOVER.
Between 9 a.m. and 12 noon, or after 5 p.m.

An early photograph of the Turkish Tom Thumb, the smallest man in the world

Sadly, the Royal Hippodrome was badly damaged and largely destroyed by one of the last World War II enemy shells fired by German long range guns during a morning rehearsal on the 18th September 1944. In the December, at a Council meeting, the Council were debating on town planning developments. Comment was made that the Royal Hippodrome could possibly have repairs to make it possible to carry on, but that it would be unwise to spend large sums of money on it, while the Surveyor said that the building was deteriorating and money available for the repairs needed to enable it to be re-opened would not be sufficient. Left as a ruin, the remaining shell of the theatre building was eventually demolished some six years later in 1951, at that time becoming a timber yard, so finally bringing an end to Dover's popular variety theatre and entertainment venue.

RAMSGATE'S LONG-ESTABLISHED CIRCUS, DRAMA AND PANTOMIME VENUE

The history of circus performances, dramatic stage plays, concerts and pantomime in Ramsgate can be traced back almost 140 years to the opening of George Sanger's Amphitheatre on Monday 23rd July 1883. At the opening, Mr. Sanger appeared on a balcony over the principal entrance in the High Street, and amidst the cheers of the large crowd assembled outside, declared the building open to the public. Shortly after the opening there were said to be over a 1,000 people already present inside.

Although essentially a circus building, it was so constructed that it could take almost any form or shape, and therefore be successfully used for opera, variety performances or drama. There were promenades on each side, and a pit promenade that was level with the stage, and when the building was floored over it was be possible to hold large Promenade Concerts. The body of the hall could also be

GEORGE SANGER'S
AMPHITHEATRE
AND
ASSEMBLY ROOMS,
RAMSGATE.
THE above GRAND ESTABLISHMENT will
POSITIVELY OPEN
On MONDAY, JULY 93rd.
For further particulars see future announcements.

Opening of the Amphitheatre in July 1883. Newspaper image © The British Library Board. All rights reserved. With thanks to The British Newspaper Archive (www.britishnewspaperarchive.co.uk).

converted for circus performances, where they could 'present the equestrian business in a manner that would meet the approbation of the Amphitheatre's Ramsgate friends.'

Overall, the Amphitheatre buildings consisted of shops with a

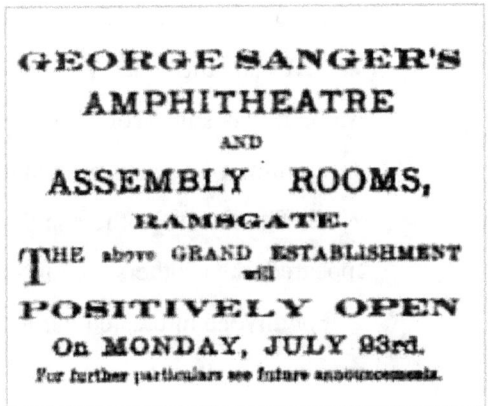

107

frontage to the High Street of 127 feet, and to George Street some 117 feet, behind which was the 2,000 seat amphitheatre; the whole block of buildings covering almost half-an-acre. It was claimed that in the event of a fire the whole audience could be evacuated through five exits in less than a minute-and-a-half. There were also fire hydrants in conspicuous places within the building. The stage area was around 2,000 sq. feet in area and it was claimed that there was not another stage in Kent of such dimensions suitable for major performances, such as ballet.

At the conclusion of Mr. Sanger's opening address, the curtain was drawn up and the whole company, including the architect, builders, surveyor and the general manager lined up on the stage. The National Anthem was sung, solo singing performances given, followed by a programme of variety entertainment in which Messrs. Ottway and Ward, The Faust Brothers and Mr. Woodhead, the "musical marvel,' appeared, the brothers creating considerable amusement.

For anyone interested in finding out more about the Amphitheatre opening there is a long and quite detailed report in the *Thanet Advertiser* of 28th July 1883.

A few months after the opening, in October 1883, George Sanger's Great Circus Company, having travelled through France, Belgium, and Holland, and having terminated their Summer Campaign in Calais, shipped from Calais to Ramsgate, ready for opening at the Ramsgate Amphitheatre on the 6th November, presenting male and female equestrians, acrobats, gymnasts, and a Host of Jolly Clowns, a stud of highly trained horses and ponies, mules and monkeys, as well as speciality artistes.

Other circus performances during the next few years highlighted acts such as Alpine Charlie and his wonderful kennel of twelve ravenous wolves, in which Charlie feeds the ravenous monsters from his naked hand. They were said to be same wolves that attacked and killed a horse at the Amphitheatre in February 1888. In June 1888, the Amphitheatre presented a spectacular pageant featuring "George and the Fiery Dragon," "The Great Ostrich Hunt" — with real ostriches, dogs and natives in true costumes — plus "Salamander the War Horse and Fire Kings."

Over the coming few years, together with the circus performances, drama seemed to be one of the great attractions at the Amphitheatre. Presented with enormous success for the Easter Holidays in March 1885 for example, was the engagement of the talented actress Miss Emma Rainbow and her powerful company in the great drama "Proved True." The dramatic presentation was pronounced by the press as one of the best Companies that have ever visited Ramsgate.

Then in October 1885, the Amphitheatre presented a sensational drama, in five acts, entitled "After Dark," which had been previously performed at the Princess' Theatre, London, to overflowing audiences for upwards of 200 nights. With new and appropriate scenery the drama introduced Charing Cross Station and Blackfriars Bridge by night, and the Underground Railway.

The Amphitheatre's success at presenting drama was claimed to be down to the great advances made in drama "realistic," and the art of scene painters, stage carpenters, etc., who had brought such a high pitch of perfection to the theatre that, while looking at a modern sensational play, it was possible to indulge in the delusion that the scenes presented were actual events of life. Ramsgate's playgoers were said to be thrilled and astonished by the most marvellous representations of shipwrecks, battles, and explosions — and even an earthquake, or the great fire scene in the presentation of "The Streets of London."

Sanger's Amphitheatre was also able to attract some of the very best actors and actresses from the London stage, such as Miss Gertrude Norman, one of the finest and most talented actress of drama, who performed throughout the week in July 1888, in the play "To the Death," a dramatised version of the celebrated novel, "Mr. Barnes of New York." She was to later become a screen writer and director for early silent films, as well as starring in some 44 films between 1911 and 1936.

Promotional poster for Aladdin& the Forty Thieves playing at Sanger's Amphitheatre in 1886

The Amphitheatre was already presenting Christmas pantomimes to Ramsgate audiences way back in the early 1880s when, for four nights in 1883, "Beauty and the Beast" was performed at three afternoon performances and an evening performance. It offered a full and efficient chorus, a troupe of lady dancers and magnificent scenery. Admission to the stalls was three shillings, the balcony one shilling and sixpence, and the gallery sixpence. The following year the pantomime was "Cinderella," which was said to be another tremendous success, while in December 1885 to January 1886, the pantomime was Aladdin and the Forty Thieves.

In January 1901 the Christmas pantomime was "Little Red Riding Hood." This ran from the 24th December 1900 to the 5th January 1901.

Looking a few years further on, the pantomime presented in January 1907 was the adventures of "Robinson Crusoe." The promotion for this included the message that the theatre was "The Finest Smoking Promenade on the Coast." Amazingly, the seat prices were still the same as for the pantomime back in 1883. The *East Kent Times and Mail* of 9th January 1907, reported that it was one of the best pantomimes that has been seen in Ramsgate.

That same year there were two Christmas pantomimes; "Babes in the Wood" from December 26th for three nights and three matinees, followed by the comic pantomime "Sinbad the Sailor" in early January 1908, both under the management of Henry Bowman.

Pantomime's were not only presented at the theatre at Christmas time. It also presented them at Easter. In April 1906 the Easter pantomime was of "Blue-Beard," which was said to be extremely light and airy, a delightful pot-pourri of catchy songs, clever dances, and amusing jokes that never allowed a moment's dullness. Large houses were delighted with the performances.

By the end of the first decade of the 1900s, the Amphitheatre was by now presenting Animated Photographs. The showing for the week commencing 25th February 1907 included vivid illustrations of the "Wreck of Berlin," with pictures said to be taken from all parts of the City. A few months later the programme comprised a colossal collection of costly cinematograms and world-famed Electric Animated Pictures, including the Wonders of Canada, the Life of Louis XIV, Jones' new motor car, Niagara, and the Sweet Suffragettes.

Opera also regularly featured. The programme for 13th to the 16th November 1907 was the magnificent opera "Merrie England," performed by The Ramsgate Operatic & Dramatic Society, which included a chorus of 60. The following week a Grand Concert Recital presented Marie Brema, the great Wagnerian singer, Jan Hambro, the famous Russian violinist, and Boris Hambourg, the celebrated cellist.

Permission to make certain structural alterations to the Amphitheatre was applied for in March 1907. It was said in the application that the plans would involve an expenditure of from £5,000 to £10,000, and the improvements would provide Ramsgate with a good-class up-to-date and modern theatre. The alterations proposed were for an extra bar to be built in the gallery, bringing the number of bars up to three, none of which could be accessed from the street without paying to go in. Part of this work was completed and it was re-opened in July, 1907.

It was around the same time that Lord George Sanger (although Sanger adopted the title Lord he was only an English showman and

An early photograph of the Palace Theatre, Ramsgate.
Source Kent County Council Libraries Registration & Archives

circus proprietor, and the son of a showman father), said he was advertising the Amphitheatre for sale, "the only reason for selling being that, as a man of eighty, he was somewhat too antique and slow for the wicked world."

A few months later Mr. Henry Bowman, who had managed the Amphitheatre for many years, announced he would cease to be connected with the theatre after January 1908, saying that the building would be entirely reconstructed and would then re-open at Easter 1908 under the title of the New Palace Theatre, and with an entirely new management.

One of his final management roles at the Amphitheatre was that of presenting the Samuel James & Newman Maurice comic Christmas pantomime "Sinbad the Sailor," each evening from Wednesday 8th January to Saturday 11th January, with a matinee performance at 2.30pm on the Saturday.

Now under the management of Mr. Charles Melvin, the fully reconstructed New Palace Theatre had its formal opening by the Mayor and Mayoress, and supported by H. H. Marks, Esq., M.P., members of the Ramsgate Town Council, and other influential residents, on Saturday 6th June, 1908, at 4 o'clock.

Following the full theatre reconstruction, including changes to entrances in the High Street and from George Street, a new foyer, additional exits for the balcony and stalls, refurbished staircases, the elevation of the balcony, the New Palace Theatre then opened for performances on Whit-Monday 1908, with a presentation of the musical comedy, "Florodora," from The Lyric Theatre, London. The piece was presented by Mr. J. Bannister Howard's principal London Company, supported by a powerful chorus and augmented orchestra.

Other changes at the Theatre provided for a spacious gallery and a roomy promenade, soundproof bars that are out of sound to the audience, easy access to seats, tasteful decorations, fireproof stage curtains, lighting effects by electric manipulation, re-painting and improvement of the entire scenery, and improvements for the convenience of the artistes.

January 1911 once again saw the presentation of "Babes in the Wood," the popular children's pantomime. This latest presentation of the pantomime contained no less than ten artistic scenes, with a special feature being made of the ballets, for which forty London dancers were engaged. Mr. Charles Kay made another of his many pantomime appearances at Kent's seaside resorts, again successfully playing the role of the Baron.

It was towards the end of 1911 that newspapers were reporting that Lord George Sanger, the famous showman who had been responsible for the building of the New Palace Theatre, had been brutally attacked and murdered at his home in Finchley, London, where he was in retirement. A very sad ending for someone who had done so much for Ramsgate.

October 1912 sees the Palace Theatre presenting a merry musical comedy, "The Colombo Girl," a pot-pourri of general light songs, dainty dances and a bevy of pretty girls in a variety of pretty dresses. There seems little doubt that over many years the residents of Ramsgate were regularly attracted to pretty girls on the stage.

Something rather different was featured in the summer of 1913 when the Palace Theatre held a "Ramsgate Ragtime" competition, with a first prize of £5 and the option of a week's engagement at the theatre. Promotion for the event said that 'The people of Ramsgate can be divided into two distinct classes this week—those who are going in for the ragtime competition at the Palace Theatre and those who are crowding in to hear them.' At the end of the week it was doubtful which was the large section, but the house was certainly packed twice nightly with competitors and judges. The press noted that 'Ramsgate's rag-timers' were toppling over one another in their anxiety to show how ragtime really should be syncopated.

The same year, the pantomime for December 1913 and into January 1914 was Lena Stepson's London Company performing "Mother Goose," the story of the wicked witch, the good fairy and the goose that laid a golden egg. This introduced 'Joey,' who was claimed to be the 'only performing goose on the stage anywhere in the world."

The ever-popular "Babes in the Wood" was once again the Christmas pantomime for six nights and three matinees in December 1915. The cast included The Aza Brothers, Little Miriam Stuart, Miss Grannie Pickford, Jen Asta and Joe spree, together with an augmented orchestra and a chorus of beautiful girls. This was followed in February 1916 by "Jack and the Beanstalk," alternatively called the Man in the Moon and the comical Old Giant Grimgruffian, with a full company of forty.

May 1915 saw the Palace Theatre again revert to its circus roots with a performance by Captain Woodward's famous sea lions in a wonderful exhibition of animal training, with the animal's juggling feats only obtained after much practice. The *East Kent Times* of Wednesday 19th May commented that 'Captain Woodward's seals are so well known in Ramsgate that they are bound to attract large audiences.'

The next few years bring "Cinderella," "Sinbad the Sailor," "Babes in the Wood," Robinson Crusoe," "Aladdin," "Dick Whittington and his Cat,"back to the Palace Theatre. Specialities at the pantomimes included The Lintons, a world renowned musical act, Mons Remo the contortionist, aerobatic dancers and the Emerald Girls.

Occasional circus performances continued at the Palace Theatre into the 1920s. One of the best circus variety shows seen in Ramsgate took place in June 1921, where the various acts included trick cyclists, a trapeze artist, clever acrobats, a trick pony, excellent musical turns and comedy.

In late February 1924 Gilbert & Sullivan's opera "The Pirates of

Penzance" continued the wide range of programmes to be performed at the Theatre, this time presented by the Ramsgate Operatic & Dramatic Society over two nights. The theatre was then closed for a couple of months to be elaborately and thoroughly improved, together with re-seating.

The opening performance of the once again refurbished theatre, variety and picture house took place on Whit-Monday afternoon and evening, with two shows taking place each day for the rest of the week. Variety performance were the chief attraction, with those appearing including Victoria Monks in her latest successes, Finlay Dunn, the piano comedian, The Sparkling Mazelles, Peels and Curtiss, Viva Daron, Frank Somers and Gordon Terry (New Zealand's singing vagabond).

The following month of July 1924 brings circus back to the theatre, with the Royal Italian Circus — who had twice appeared at Buckingham Palace by Royal Command — presenting a delightful entertainment that was suitable for both young and old in which there were some particularly clever turns, notably those by Giro and Toni who presented an oriental act, Mademoiselle Mona Connor's bare back riding and some remarkable activities by horses, dogs, donkeys and Maymo, the Burmese elephant.

Two well-known and famous exponents of the art of laughter made their appearance at the Palace Theatre in November 1925, when Lew Lake (the English comic actor, writer, producer and theatre manager) and Renée Reel (a musical comedy and variety comedian) took to the stage in their revue "My Erb." The promotion for the show claimed they were known throughout the country as the cream of their profession. As a producer, Lew Lake worked closely with the husband-and-wife team of Arthur Lucan and Kitty McShane in the 1920s, and devised several of their shows featuring the couple as "Old Mother Riley and Daughter".[

Something rather different and quite new came to the Palace Theatre in June 1927 when the revue depicted the Kentucky cotton fields, reminiscent of the slavery days of America where the slaves learn of the death of their master, after which they are sold by auction. Following scenes show them being purchased by a theatrical producer who, seeing talent in them, decides to have them educated for the stage. They finally appear as a successful old time minstrel troupe.

As the Palace Theatre moved into the 1930 the variety shows gave way to an ever increasing showings of big cinema films. This often meant three days of films and three days of variety, with perhaps a concert on the Sunday. Films shown over the weeks and moths of the 1930 enable Ramsgate filmgoers to see all the leading male and female film stars of the time. Too many to mention them all, but favourites included Gracie Fields, Ginger Rogers, Kay Francis, Laurel & Hardy, Charlie Chaplin, Margaret Lockwood, Henry Fonda, Maureen O'Sullivan, Bette Davies, Judy Garland, Boris Karloff, Shirley Temple and Mickey Rooney.

Towards the end of the 1930s, The Palace Theatre started introducing "Search for Talent" entertainment evenings, inviting contestants that could sing, dance, recite, play an instrument, to come along to preliminary heats and the final rounds. No-one was barred, and judging was by public acclaim, with the competition being run by Tony Gerrard, the well-known Cockney comedian. Winners of the talent competitions received a quite sizeable amount of money. Mr Gerrard said that some of the most accomplished entertainers he had ever heard had been discovered in Ramsgate.

A return to circus acts came to the Theatre in May 1938 when the Royal Bengal Circus, presenting the world's greatest animal acts, arrived in Ramsgate. Attractions in the circus performances included forest-bred lions, Himalayan bears, Polar bears, a boxing kangaroo, musical elephants, sea lions, high-school horses, as well as bare-back riders and jovial clowns.

December 1938 and January 1939 brings two more pantomimes to the Palace Theatre with, firstly "Robinson Crusoe," followed a few weeks later by "Aladdin" which featured magnificent scenes of Oriental splendour. The plotting and scheming of Abanazar and the Grand Vizier were carried on through scene after scene until the Emperor's lovely Palace gardens and the story finally ended in Aladdin's beautiful Palace.

A completely new policy was introduced at the Theatre in July 1939, with the beginning of twice nightly performances of

Palace Theatre

Tel. 31   RAMSGATE.   Tel. 31
BALEXCRO THEATRES, LTD.

MONDAY, AUGUST 1st, 1938

6·30   TWICE NIGHTLY 8·40

Full Star Variety Programme

INCLUDING

Bennett and Williams

Hamilton   Conrad

Eddie   Bayes

PRICES OF ADMISSION
(Including Tax)

Front Stalls 1/6   Front Circle 1/6
(Bookable)   (Bookable)
Centre Stalls 1/-   Back Circle 1/-
(Bookable)   (Bookable)
Back Stalls 9d.   Balcony 6d.

Programme   ·   ·   ·   Price 1d.

LAST TRAINS FROM RAMSGATE

Weekdays—To Margate   10·32   Sundays—To Minster   10·55
         Minster   Canterbury
         Sandwich 10·10
         Canterbury   Sundays—To Sandwich   10·10

                               Buses wait for 2nd house patrons
Sundays—To Margate   10·55   for Margate, Broadstairs and St
         „   11·15   Peter's (Also Cliffs End, Minster
         „   12·25   Sandwich. **Saturdays only**

Printers—W. H. BLIGH & Co., Ltd. Ramsgate

Full Star Variety Programme for the Palace Theatre dated August 1st 1938

NEXT WEEK:
Harry Hemsley, Beryl Beresford, The Great Garcias

CHOCOLATES, CIGARETTES and ICES
can be obtained from the Attendants.

WILLIAM HENSHALL Ltd., brings you

"RED HOT AND BLUE MOMENTS"

Programme

A Bell will be rung in the Bars One Minute before commencing

Overture

1	Swing	Evelyn Taylor Jnr. and Henshall's Young Ladies
2	Lovers Wanted	Sid Field, Alex Foster and Evelyn Taylor
3	Vanity	Nanette with Henshall's Young Ladies
4	Learning to Play Golf	Sid Field and Alex Foster
5	William Breach	Will Sing
6	Amy Drinkwater	Sid Field, Alex Foster, Albert Clarke and Lillian Trever
7	Rhapsody in Jazz	The Ted Lewis Swing Band conducted by Evelyn Taylor with Henshall's Young Ladies.

Intermission

Selection—"Musical Comedy Switch" ... Henry Hall.
By the Palace Theatre Orchestra
(Under the direction of Mr. FRANK WALLER)

The Pianette "Minipiano" used in the "Rhapsody in Jazz" Scene with the Ted Lewis Band by courtesy of W. C. Ravenscroft & Sons, Ltd. London.

A Bell will be rung in the Bars One Minute before the next Act

8	Buenos Aires	Ted Lewis' Rhythm Accordianists with Evelyn Taylor, Nanette and Henshall's Young Ladies.
9	William Breach	Will Sing Again.
10	Idols	Sid Field, Lillian Trever, Alex Foster and Evelyn Taylor.
11	Nanette	On Her Toes
12	Sid Goes to Heaven	Sid Field, Alex Foster, Evelyn Taylor and Henshall's Young Ladies.
13	Foster and Clarke	Quick Wits.
14	The Lederers	Clever with Clubs
15	Almost a Musician	Sid Field, Alex Foster and William Breach.
16	Finale	The Company.

GOD SAVE THE KING.

Programme subject to slight alteration.

| Stage Director Musical Director | For William Henshall, Ltd. | Rex Snelgrove Freddie Waite |

Although this is not a CONTINUOUS PERFORMANCE patrons arriving late may enter providing SEATS ARE AVAILABLE and remain to see the whole programme.

Promotional poster for Aladdin& the Forty Thieves playing at Sanger's Amphitheatre in 1886

both cinema and the Full Star Variety Programmes that had become a regular feature at the Palace. This change was made in order to meet the convenience of patrons that came from outlying districts, and who, sometimes found difficulty in getting to Ramsgate for the rise of the curtain in a once-nightly performance.

An organisation was also set-up so that parties of friends from around the district could be accommodated not only with seats at the theatre, but also transport from and to their homes at an inclusive charge. This new policy proved a great boon, with parties accommodated from outlying Ramsgate, and from Margate, Broadstairs and even St. Nicholas-at-Wade coming in to see the weekly variety programmes that were attracting audiences into the town.

One of the programmes for the variety shows at the Palace in 1938 (reproduced) features Sid Field, the British comedian, who was known for having his audiences roaring with laughter and, as one reviewer commented, they were literally "falling of their seats with laughter." He was particularly loved for his routines involving a naive approach to the billiards table and the golf course, Unusual among comedy performers, his act was a wide mix of characters and impersonations at a time when most variety acts were said to be 'one trick ponies.'

Another 20th century music hall comedian and radio presenter to appear at the Palace theatre in 1938 was Harry Hemsley. He his often remembered for his popular radio show the "Ovaltiney's Concert Party, which spawned its own comic magazine: Ovaltiney's Own Comic.

Local talent shows at the Theatre continued in the 1940s, with Hughie Green's "Opportunity Knocks" looking for the stars of tomorrow that might be found in Ramsgate. As before, cash prizes were offered to winners.

Regular presentations of well-known plays were re- introduced at the Theatre after the end of World War II, with the Palace putting on "Arsenic and Old Lace," "Pygmalion," "The Christmas Carol" by Charles Dickens, "The Winslow Boy," and the "The Poltergeist" by Bernard Shaw.

Ramsgate's Palace Theatre managed to continue with some top-star variety performances into the 1950s by bringing in popular comedians such as Max Miller, Peter Sellers, Monsewer Eddie Gray, and Wee Georgie Wood, as well as putting on "Thanks for the Memory" old troupers shows which again brought back many of the

121

country's older music hall artistes, such as G. H. Elliott, Ella Shields, Randolph Sutton and Billy Danvers to perform their old melodies and songs which had lived through to generations.

The Theatre also moved towards a more saucy French atmosphere in early 1950s, putting on a revue entitled "French Capers," described as having all the elements of a Continental atmosphere, and containing no fewer than a dozen scenes, including a French bubble dance. A few weeks later the Palace Theatre presented the record breaking novelty road show "Nudes Parisienne."

Then in July 1952, The Palace Theatre, described at the time as one of the oldest theatres in the country, changed hands. The new owner, who also purchased Ramsgate's King's Theatre and the Ramsgate Picture House, was the Highland Trust Development Co. Ltd. No changes were made to the rest of the season's variety shows booked for the Palace during the rest of the year.

Ramsgate's Palace Theatre finally closed on the 29th October 1960, after a wide and varied existence dating back to Sanger's Amphitheatre, which had opened way back in 1883. The last performance was an X feature film "Never take sweets

Max Miller, the often very risque comedian, who appeared at the Palace Theatre in the 1950s

122

from a stranger." The manager of the Palace, Mr. G. V. Jennings, stayed with the Highland Trust Development, who continued to run the King's Cinema and the New Picture House in Ramsgate

Planning permission was given for the reconstruction of the Palace Theatre and Sanger's Hotel and for it to be convert into a two-storey multiple store for Fine Fare, at that time one of the country's major supermarket chains. The chain was sold in the mid 1900s, firstly becoming Gateway and then Somerfield. The applicants were the owners of the block, Central Commercial Properties Ltd.

20TH CENTURY THEATRE AND SPACIOUS CINEMA BUILT IN RAMSGATE

A proposal to construct the latest and most comfortable Cinematograph and Vaudeville Theatre in Thanet was set out by The Ramsgate and District Popular Amusement Company Ltd. in an advertisement placed in the *East Kent Times and Mail* of Wednesday 18th May 1910. Capital was to be raised by issuing 1,400 Preference shares of £1 each.

The site of the proposed entertainment hall and theatre was between 6,500 and 7,000 square feet and right in the centre of Ramsgate, with access from King Street and the Market Place, but also from Abbot's Hill. Originally, the proposed site was where the Red Lion Inn (dating back to the 1650s and said to be the oldest surviving pub in Ramsgate) had provided good stabling for between sixty and seventy horses, plus lock-up coach houses. The Inn had advertised neat post-chaise, able horses, and careful drivers to any part of the kingdom.

Entrance to the new hall was to be situated so as to attract not only residents but also the many thousands of visitors that flocked to Ramsgate during the summer months. Money raised by the share issue would be used to obtain a 21 year lease of the site at a rental of £40 per annum, for the construction and fitting out, seating and employment of the management.

In the following week's newspapers appearing after the capital raising, there were further details set out by the Ramsgate and District Popular Amusement Company Ltd. In their follow-up report the directors said that they had been surprised and gratified by the response to the invitation to invest in the company, and that almost all the shares had been taken up by local residents. They pointed out that the picture theatre was so far almost unknown in Great Britain, and that animated picture entertainment was still in its infancy, it just needed organising capacity and the co-operation of capital to create the solid foundations.

It was also noted that the cine-variety concept was a class of entertainment so cheap to start, so cheap to run, and so easily sited near where people lived, that wherever they have been opened — especially in America — they had been instantaneously successful. This investment in the Ramsgate Cinematograph and Vaudeville Theatre would therefore be a most lucrative investment.

By August 1910 the contractor, Mr. A. E. Goodbourn, had already commenced building Ramsgate's new picture theatre. Designed by Mr. H. Bertram Langham, the building had brick walls, would be of substantial character with attractive elevations, have a high pitched roof, a balcony, with patrons able to enter a tiny foyer at street level and from there ascend a staircase to the stalls foyer. A further staircase led up to the theatre balcony. The rear of the building housed an impressive six stained-glass windows.

Just two months later the Ramsgate and District Popular Amusement Company Ltd., announced that the "King's Electric Theatre," at Market Place and Abbot's Hill, and the latest and most comfortable Cinematograph Vaudeville Theatre in Thanet, under Managing Director Reginald V. Crow, would open to the public with a high-class variety programme commencing on Monday 7th November 1910.

A display advertisement in The *East Kent Times and Mail* of Wednesday 9th November 1910, highlighted that 'Jury's Imperial

Pictures' (acknowledged to be the finest animated pictures ever seen in Ramsgate) would be showing at King's Electric Theatre during the week commencing November 7th, together with Ramsgate's favourite baritone, Percy E. Wright, and The Musical Bon-Bons, a novelty musical and dancing speciality.

The following week, advertising for the theatre now included the message 'This Theatre is voted by public and press, the most comfortable, safe, and luxurious Cinematograph and Vaudeville Theatre in Thanet.' Alongside Percy E. Wright, the programme now additionally included 'The starring engagement for the week of The Irish-Americans, Shamus & Kittie, in their high-class comedy, vocal and dancing speciality, "Merry Minglings."

By the middle of December 1910, little more than a month after the theatre's opening, the newspaper advertising was again amended to add 'Travel, Instructive, Dramatic and Comic Films to suit all tastes, including local pictures taken by our operator.' There was also the message 'This Theatre is warm and comfortable — No draughts around your legs here!' The variety entertainment for the week was La Sarella, the dainty barefoot and legmania dancer, and Billy Gartel, musical comedian and raconteur.'

Just a week later, the programme offered specially selected animated pictures, and the Animatophone Singing Pictures, including their famous production of the popular Opera, "Il Travatore." By special request the local pictures being shown were 'A day with the Ramsgate Fishermen.' The variety acts for the week were Joe Cookson, the world's premier ventriloquist, and The Clancy Girls, singers and dancers from the principal London Halls.

To end the year, The King's Electric Theatre, was filled to overflowing during the week commencing 26th December, 1910, with an excellent programme of pictures and varieties. The miniature Pierrot Entertainment, presented by The Forders and their Lilliputian Stars, was a great success. Glen Alva, the comedienne and dancer, also had a warm reception, whilst Bella White was a clever chic comedian and dancer. The films included "The Taking of Saragossa," "The Missing Bridegroom." "Painless Extraction," and "Who's Who."

The second decade of the 1900s continued with the ongoing success of the King's Electric Theatre, with attractive and interesting programmes of films, and the varied selection of variety acts and evening entertainment. In March 1911, the entertainment included Will Powell, vocalist and champion clog dancer who, with the management arranged a Clog Dancing Competition, open to all amateurs in Kent, ladies or gentlemen. No one barred. Heats were arrange nightly, with a final on the Friday night. The winner received a gold centre medal and the offer of a week's salaried engagement. Will Powell was the judge.

In a programme in June, the star artists were Tom Delaware, in his famous impersonations of lady Vaudeville stars; Ray Glynne, a novel musical and dancing act, and J. P. Boston, an English and Irish variety entertainer in his speciality — Stick manipulation, Clog and Pump dancing. At a children's matinee on the Saturday (17th June) a free gift of a Coronation Badge, containing a real photo of H. M. The King, was given to every child paying for admission.

Hot weather in August 1911 saw the management of the King's present each lady patron who purchased a programme with a fan to keep them cool. Shamus and Kittie, the Irish comedians and dancers also returned to the theatre, again being accorded a hearty reception.

During the year, the showing of films changed by arrangement with Jury's Imperial Pictures Lt., to The Kingscope Animated PIctures. The films shown changed twice weekly, with the variety entertainment continuing with ever-varied programmes. October 1911, for example, had Spangellette and the Joy Wheel Dogs, The Great Platter, an American Comedy Juggler, and Tom Carney, a character comedian and dancer.

February 1912 sees The Lorettes at the King's Theatre in their daring and sensational act on the double trapeze. Adding to the evenings entertainment were Norman M. Lee, the comedian with the board and easel, and Leoville, the greatest of all lady wire walkers in the most up-to-date wire act in Britain, assisted by funny Scotchman, Sandy M'Gregor.

Performing animals and birds were much to the fore at the King's Theatre during 1912, with a smart variety turn in May again provided by Madame Spangellette's clever dogs. This bright troupe of canines performed many clever feats, such as jumping and diving, as well as playing a game of football. More clever dogs followed in the September, this time presented by Corbin's high leaping and boxing dogs.

By the June of 1912, the name of the theatre had changed and was now being promoted in newspaper advertising as 'The King's Theatre of Varieties,' reflecting the ever wider range of, quite often, rather extravagant artists and acts appearing on the bill.

Certainly one of the more extravagant animal acts to appear at the theatre came along in October that year, when Leoni Clarke presented his 200 performing animals. The animals included cats, rabbits, monkeys and assorted other highly intelligent animals that performed some amazing feats. Amongst these was a musical monkey that played the mandoline, a cat that performed with a whistle, and a rabbit which banged a tambourine. The cats were said to be particularly sagacious, walking over mice, canaries and pigeons with the greatest concern. Two of the clever cats also participated in an exciting boxing match, whilst another one made a parachute descent. Another feature of the entertainment was a guinea pig express.

Later in October 1912, Mons. Roelgin appeared with his marvellous parrots performing some clever activities, among them being the driving of a motor car, the riding of a tricycle, and riding on a swing, altogether the most wonderful display of intelligence ever

The East Kent Times. Wednesday 23rd October 1912. Newspaper image © The British Library Board. All rights reserved. With thanks to The British Newspaper Archive (www. britishnewspaperarchive.co.uk).

seen, especially the parrot with a human brain. Adding comedy to the evening on the same bill, was the welcome return of Charles Kay, Kent's favourite comedian, who was warmly applauded for his song "The Vicar of Slopton," and Miss Lola Trent (his wife) who created much merriment in "Billy the Broker's Man."

Fitted in between the animal acts in October was Mrs. Victor's celebrated "Baby Brigade," direct from the Lyceum Theatre, London. This consisted of ten talented small children in different song and dance scenes. The children were said to have already performed twice before the Royal Family. Also on the same bill were Tommy Banks, a popular comedian and dancer, and May Daulton, a comedienne and an 'expert' dancer.

One of the most mystifying acts that ever presented in Ramsgate, or for the matter in any other town, drew large audiences to the King's Theatre of Varieties in May 1913. Billed as "Yuma. What is it?" The act commenced with a comparatively small box (28 inches long, 17 inches wide and 15 inches high) being brought on stage and laid on a carpet. As a lady in Oriental costume removed the lid it suddenly opened to expose an automaton-like figure stretched out on the ground, clad in the uniform of German cuirassier (16th century armoured cavalry equipped with a cuirass, sword, and pistols). When lifted upright with helmet affixed, the apparent automaton, standing some seven feet high, walked with a doll-like stilled mechanical gait to the front of the stage and drew a sword. Electric wires were attached to its body, and flashes of light marked every movement.

Another and non-collapsible box was then brought out and, after being touched by a female magician, the automaton tumbled in, doubled over, tucked its legs in and the box closed and placed in an iron crate and suspended with ropes and pulleys in mid-air. To the question 'What is Yuma' the box then burst open to reveal, not an automaton, but a big, handsome, heavily built athlete attired as Mephistopheles, who then performed a trapeze act, concluding with a marvellous contortionist performance — and rightfully receiving a great ovation.

In August 1913 the King's Theatre announced that, in addition to a new system of ventilation that they had invested in, they had now also installed a gigantic Punkah Fan - as widely used in India - in the balcony, making this the coolest place in the building.

The starring engagement of what was said to be the most expensive variety act as having ever visited Ramsgate and promoted as such in the local newspaper advertising, took place in the February of 1914, when "The Five X Rays, the Mad Athletes," performed at the Theatre.

This was followed in April of the same year by Madame Roseau's trained dogs, described as the smallest toy dogs to be performing on the stage. Topping the bill at the King's Theatre, they provided a particularly popular turn, with Tiny, "the celebrated globe walker on the high wire," being an especial favourite. On the first three nights the programme also included the star picture "Raised from the Ranks," a spirited military drama of much topical interest. For the second three evenings the first-class film was "The Battle of Elderbusb Gulch," said to be an exciting pictorial record of war in the wild and woolly west.

The following month the Theatre received packed houses to view the great screen production of "The Three Musketeers," claimed as a remarkable specimen of the cinematograph art, with no expense spared in its production, and the settings being on a luxurious scale, with each scene being most carefully thought out.

Large audiences were again attracted to the popular pleasure and picture palace theatre in June 1914 when the main film for the first three nights of the week was "The Adventure of the Copper Beeches," No.8 in the Sherlock Holmes series. Later in the week the screenings included an excellent story of the American Civil War. The between film entertainment was provided by the Society Quartette, a group of clever vaudeville entertainers.

By now, advertising and promotion were simply under the name of the King's Theatre, having been shortened from the King's Theatre of Varieties. The variety element of the evenings was also being gradually reduced in favour of an increased number of films (up to four each evening) and maybe just one or two variety turns. The message coming from the management now featured as 'As far as cinematography is concerned, the King's management continues to lead the way.'

Featured in between films, including a review of the British Fleet, at Spithead, by his Majesty the King, the programme for the week commencing 17th August, 1914, was the re-engagement of Mr. Arthur J. Hill, an unusually clever ventriloquist who introduced "Wally — the almost human automaton," a young gentleman that provided a great source of amusement as he resisted the efforts of a commmmissionaire trying to remove him from the stage.

The very popular managing director of the King's Theatre, Mr R.

Crow, joined the motor transport section of the Colours in November 1915. His wife Mrs R. V. Crow was appointed as acting managing director, although his name continued to be promoted in advertising. The theatre programmes were now predominately films only. Charlie Chaplin, the Keystone Cops and Buster Keaton films always attracted large audiences.

For much of the second half of the 1920s the King's Theatre had become a full-time cinema. Adventurous and exciting variety acts of all kinds were now a thing of the past, and this was the way it was to remain without any real change until the 1970s when, firstly the name changes to simply 'Kings,' and then in August 1978, following its acquisition by the Classic Cinemas chain in late June, to 'Kings Cinema. The cinema was also re-decorated.

This put the Classic and Kings Cinema in Ramsgate under one management and with the need to recruit additional staff, advertising for many months, apparently without a great deal of success.

Following the takeover, the Kings Cinema embarked on the showing over many months of a succession of erotic films such as 'Emanuelle,' 'Emanuelle II,' 'Black Emanuelle, White Emanuelle,' 'Emanuelle in Tokyo,' 'A young Emanuelle after dark,' 'Erotic young lovers,' 'French undressing,' 'Confessions of a sexy photographer,' 'Experiment in sexual inhibitions,' 'The virgin wife,' 'Erotic adventures of Pinocchio,' and 'Confessions of a window cleaner.'

Then in November 1982, the cinema had to close when its rectifier burnt out. As Classic Cinemas also owned the Classic Cinema just along the road it was decided not to spend further money on the Kings Cinema and it remained closed — and sadly never re-opened.

It was later converted and, from 1989 to 2016, used as Kings Church. When the Church moved out of the building in 2016 it was put up for sale, becoming a Hindu Temple in 2017

MUSIC HALL AND VARIETY THEATRE ARRIVE IN SHEERNESS

Like most of the other coastal towns in Kent that London, the Medway towns and even further afield, had visitors regularly travelling to by steamer and rail for day trips and holidays during the 1860s, 1870s and 1880s, Sheerness had begun looking to establish its own venue that could host a wide mix of concerts, drama, music hall and variety shows, opera, musical evenings, pantomime, dancing and public meetings.

Planning and building of a large public hall to encompass all these activities commenced in the late 1860s and was fully built by the end of 1869, with the Victoria Hall then being formerly opened on the 26th January 1870 with a banquet attended by a few hundred leading dignitaries from Sittingbourne and Sheerness plus, as the *Sheerness Times and Guardian*, of the 5th February reported "a certain clan that could afford to be present."

Erected on the corner of Broadway and Trinity Road, The Victoria Hall and theatre was capable of seating more than a 1,200 people in the main body of the hall and gallery. Chairs and stools in the hall were divided into three blocks, the entrance being from two side doors to the body of the building, while access to the reserved seats and dress circle was by the two side doors on the right hand side of the hall. The entrance to the gallery was up stone steps just inside the front lobby, and entirely distinct from any other part. In fact, the whole of the arrangements for the comfort and convenience of those who patronised the splendid building was said to be excellent.

The main entrance to the building was lit by two elegant lamps, "Victoria Hall" being inscribed upon them, denoting that though the people of Sheerness were isolated from the main-land, the name of her Most Gracious Majesty the Queen had not been forgotten by them, hence her name was given to the hall by her most loyal Sheerness subjects.

A tessellated pavement (tessellated flooring is made up of three components; the tile pattern itself, a tile border which frames the pattern, and a tile filler which acts as a buffer between the border and the edge of the floor), in the front lobby of the building, was said to be viewed with admiration by a great many and, while much attention had been paid to accommodation and stability, 'the decoration and ornamentation could be placed to be consistent with the building's utility.' Another thing worth noting was the establishment of a cloak-room at the side of the lobby.

Opening for public performances took place a week later on Wednesday 2nd February, 1870, commencing with a Grand Concert in which the doors were thrown open to the 'high and low, rich and poor.' Seats in the dress circle were priced at 3s. 6d, with gallery seats available at 6d. Reserved seats in the hall were filled with the principal tradesmen and inhabitants of the town, together with some gentry from Sittingbourne. Both the main hall and gallery were crowded, with at least a 1,000 patrons being present. It was reported that this was 'the largest number ever collected at an in-door entertainment in the annals of Sheerness history.'

The staging in the hall was generally well admired and it was apparent that the accommodation behind the stage wall was all that could be desired, the performers said to be appearing and disappearing with evident ease and comfort. On each side of the stage there was a large room, furnished with tables and chairs, in which there was every convenience for the comfort of the artistes engaged.

The concert was announced to commence at eight o'clock, and at five minutes past that hour the members of the Royal Engineers' String Band, appeared upon the stage amid great applause, and in a masterly manner played Rossini overture "Otello." A range of other pieces were also played by them during the evening, together with piano, flute and cornet soloists, male and female solo singers. A particularly novel part of the evening came when Herr Meyer Lutz proved himself the master of the piano in splendid style when, to the astonished audience, he played the National Anthem, with variations, with his left hand only, receiving a unanimous encore.

The following ten months following the opening were largely very successful, with the taste for entertainments in Kent being of an attractive nature — at a moderate price — and growing year by year; Sheerness being no exception. In December 1870 the press reported that the Victoria Hall had only been open for ten months but had been filled comfortably a great many times. Indeed, had even been too small at times to admit all those that wished to be present.

One of the more interesting or notable presentations in the Theatre during the first years included a Japanese Troupe in September 1871. Acts appearing on stage were a lady rope and wire walker, Tommy the wolf, a 30 ft. ladder balancer, a tub and door spinner, a pole and bamboo act, screen and umbrella spinning and butterfly fanning, plus 'novel feats never attempted by any other performers.'

The first pantomime to be presented at the Victoria Hall was in February 1873 and featured the Grand Comic Pantomime, "Goody two-shoes," with new scenery painted by Mr. Richard Douglas of the National Standard Theatre and elegant new costumes. The pantomime was arranged by Miss Sarah Thorne, the manageress of the Margate Theatre, and her dramatic company. She also appeared each evening in a specially arranged comedietta — a short comic stage/musical production.

VICTORIA HALL PUT UP FOR AUCTION

In August 1873 the Victoria Hall was put up for auction. The Auction Notice said that the Hall was capable of seating a near 1,300 people and also housed The Victoria Working Men's club, the Literary Institute and the Sheppey Billiards Club. The advertisement stated that the Hall had a frontage to the Broadway of 110 feet, and 128 feet to Trinity Road. The whole building contained an area of nearly 14,000 superficial feet. The estimated rental was £200. 10s. per annum.

Two months later the Victoria Hall was advertising a Grand Concert by the Comyn Band, complete with songs, ballads and band performances, including "I wandered on the mountain side," "I love my love," "The bold fisherman," "Tell me, Mary," "The British Tar," "Sing, sweet bird," and "That's where you make the mistake."

June 1874 sees Vance's Varieties at the Hall. Claimed to be recognised by Their Royal Highnesses the Prince and Princess of Wales, as the most refined 'Melange d'Enjoument' extant, and one that afforded real enjoyment to the audience. Artistes in Vance's Concert Party included Kate Allwood, a soubrette, Miss Ellen Allwood, comedienne, Mr Alfred Velma, vocal comedian, and an all-star cast.

The music was said to be 'original and pretty, the words funny, yet would not cause a blush to the most fastidious.'

The Victoria Hall was once again put up for auction in July 1879. This time the advertisement noted that the building still held not only the Victoria Working Men's Club and the Literary Institute, but the Masonic Lodge as well. It commented that the Hall was in a central position in the populous and improving Town of Sheerness-on-Sea, and now had an income of £321.

Varity shows, concerts, opera, military band performances and pantomimes continued through much of the remainder of the 19th century and, although there was a large degree of success, there were also letters to the local paper complaining about the lack of interest in some events where fewer than 300 people were in the auditorium.

This could be one of the reasons why the Victoria Hall was once more put up for auction in September 1897. It stated that the venue, together with a plot of building land, attracted a revenue of upwards of £300 per annum. Interestingly this was less than the stated rental some 18 years earlier.

However, these problems didn't appear to have an impact on the range of variety, concert, pantomime and other entertainments to be seem at the Hall during the late 1880s and 1890s. Comic Spectacular Pantomimes were still a feature, with "Whittington and his Cat" being the pantomime presented at the end of December 1879. Again, magnificent scenery, new and gorgeous dresses and sparkling music were on offer.

In 1900 the pantomime presented for two nights on January 18th and 19th was the colossally spectacular "Sinbad the Sailor," in which the scenes included operatic, burlesque and dramatic artistes.

A whole range of one, two, three of more days of variety, dramatic, operatic and other entertainment continued at the Victoria Hall during 1901 and through 1902. Regular presentations of Gilbert and Sullivan's operas, including "Trial by Jury," and "H.M.S. Pinafore also took place in the early years of the 1900s. The Hall also first started to show animated pictures in 1902.

An enormous attraction for one night only was presented by the Livermore Brothers in October 1902 with their only and original show the "Court Minstrels." This included charming minstrel ballads, up-to-date jokes, screaming burlesque, the World Champion Dancers, altogether forming 'the most remarkable entertainment ever put before the public.'

OLD TOWN CLOCK INSTALLED IN THE VICTORIA HALL TOWER

Then, in October 1903 it was reported that the old town clock was being renovated and would then be installed in the tower at the Victoria Hall. It was hoped this could be illuminated, but the Surveyor told the Council that owing to the condition of the dials, an expense of £20 was entailed, and there would no money left for the illumination when the clock was installed. The clock's installation in the tower caused a great deal of comment and some anger in the town.

At the end of October 1903 four nights of H. Deniss-Roberts' Edison's Animatograph, exhibiting the finest selection of pictures ever taken, was a major special attraction at the Victoria Hall, coming direct from the London Hippodrome. Included in the evening was the "Greatest American Mystery" and "Phroso, the Mechanical Doll."

Sheerness benefitted from a new electric tram service

Continuing the Hall's regular programme of pantomime's, the Christmas pantomime in December 1903 was "Cinderella." Claimed to be the most gorgeous pantomime ever toured, the front seats were priced at 2s. with seats in the main body of the Hall at 1s. Children half-price.

RENAMED THE VICTORIA PALACE THEATRE

After the pantomime ended in December 1903, the Victoria Hall was to go through a period of upheaval and change, initially with extensive alterations and the seating (now arranged on a slope) and lighting undergoing a vast improvement. Further improvements planned, included raising the floor, erecting boxes, and placing tip-up chairs throughout the building. It was also announced that as from January 1904 the Hall was to be used as a variety theatre and was being renamed the Victoria Palace Theatre and would be presenting the finest entertainment in the county.

In justifying the changes it was stated that Sheerness, with a population of some 20,000 people, a combination of naval, military, and civilians, required a place of amusement for the ongoing development of the town. Sheerness at this time was also benefitting from a new electric tram service.

The newly named Victoria Palace Theatre opened in January 1904 with a Grand and Sensational Opening programme with the chief amongst them being the wonderful acrobatic performance of the "Three Guitanos." Their feats were described as the most remarkable ever put before a Sheerness audience, and the applause was frequent during their appearance on the stage. A sketch presented by the Carpenters was also excellent, and the antics of Squibs, the boy comedian, kept the company in a state of merriment. Also on the programme were American jugglers, comedians, male and female singers and dancers.

Excellent variety programmes continued to be put on in February and March 1904. An interesting new venture in the March saw the Theatre organise a cake walking competition with a first prize of £2. 2s. and handsome iced cake. A prize of 10s. 6d. was offered for the best costume, and a further prize of 10s. 6d. for the funniest couple. The then proprietor of the Theatre, Mr. Alexandroff, invited 40 children from the Minster Workhouse to attend the matinee performance. Before departing, at the conclusion of the performance, each child received a bun and an orange from the Management.

In April 1904, the proprietor applied to the Council to remove the prohibition on the sale and consumption of liquor in the Theatre while performances were being held. Council for Mr. Alexandroff said that he had yet to make a profit and had lost a considerable amount of money. He could not continue to do that. If the licence was granted it would enable him to cover all expenses at events. Unfortunately the prohibition was not removed and, by the end of April 1904, the Theatre had been closed.

The following month, a new proprietor of the Theatre, Mr. Dorling, announced that he intended to carry on the business under the name of the 'Sheerness Variety Theatre,' varying the performances occasionally between variety, musical comedies and dramas. He also submitted a plan to the Council asking to make some slight alterations to the building.

THEATRE CHANGES ITS NAME TO THE HIPPODROME

Just one year later it was announced in the *Sheerness Times Guardian* of 15th April 1905, that the Victoria Hall was thereafter to be known as the Hippodrome. Other than the change of name, performances at the Theatre continued much the same as before.

A return visit of the pantomime "Aladdin" was presented at the Theatre in March 1906, attracting large audiences and 'affording delight to crowds of people at the music hall' and attracting rounds of applause. The *Sheerness Times Guardian* of the 10th March 1906 noted that 'Mr. Dan Thomas and the various artistes who are associated with him its presentation have every reason to congratulate themselves on the return visit.'

The following month the entertainment attracting large houses at the Hippodrome was the wizard of hypnotism Ahrensmeyer, who accomplished strange deeds to be performed by the subjects he chose

145

and practised on from the audience, arousing much wonder and mirth in the auditorium. Other artistes in the programme included Teddy the well-known whistler, Maria Blythe, a sentimental singer, and the Sisters Belmont who gave clever expositions of clog, top-boot and sand dancing.

Following a visit to the Hippodrome by the Chairman of the London Alhambra and a number of first-class business men during May 1906, the Chairman of the Hippodrome announced that the businessmen had made a proposal to spend a good many thousands of pounds to make the music hall a credit to the town. The alterations planned included the conversion of buildings on the corner of Trinity Road into shops, and the erection of shelters for people waiting outside the Theatre to enter. The driving force behind the alterations was the Chairman of the London Alhambra.

On the basis that at least £8,000 would be spent to improve the Theatre, a submission to the Council to grant the long-requested alcohol licence, was finally approved in September 1906, although not without much discussion, debate, argument and adjournments.

Coming towards the end of the first decade of the 20th century, the Hippodrome continued with a varied programme of dramas, variety, music hall, bands and, in the week commencing June 28th, 1909, presented the first Sheerness appearance of the popular favourite London comedienne and burlesque artiste, Miss Billie Barlow. This was followed in July 1990 by Mr. T. G. Transfield's Comedy Circus which included performing ponies, mules, donkeys, dogs and "Rabbits" the clown, plus a company of capable performing artistes.

A few weeks later a first-class variety entertainment was provided for patrons of the music hall. The programme opened with Tom Parker, a burly comedian who gave a funny version of a married lady's troubles. His appearance in petticoats alone was enough to evoke much mirth. Also on the bill was Clack and Clack, two very clever lady barrel jumpers who performed some astonishing feats.

OWNERSHIP CHANGES TO SOUTHEND-ON-SEA THEATRE COMPANY

By now the Hippodrome was regularly showing short films as part of their evening entertainments

THE NEW HIPPODROME,
BROADWAY, SHEERNESS.
PROPRIETORS ... ... THE SOUTHEND-ON-SEA THEATRE Co., Ltd.

MONDAY, July the 5th, 1909,
AND DURING THE WEEK.
TWICE NIGHTLY AT 7 and 9.

Special and Important Engagement of Mr. T. G. TRANSFIELD, the well-known Circus Proprietor, with his

. . COMEDY CIRCUS . .

The Company includes —

THE WOELLHAFS, American Vaudeville Artistes, in their great Comedy Act.

G. W. FOSTER, the Popular Comedian.

BAKER and DE SALES, in a Smart Singing, Dancing, and Eccentric Comedy Act.

HIPPODROME PICTURES, with Latest Films.

MISS ROSE DELLA, Comedienne.

"RABBIT," the Popular Clown of Sheerness, with his Comical Donkey "Tommy."

THE THREE TRANSFIELDS, daughters of T. G. Transfield, in their Musical Speciality.

The Sensational Comedy Waiters, THE PAULASTOS, America's Greatest Acrobatic Eccentrics.

Advertisement in the Sheerness Times and General Advertiser. July 3rd 1909. Newspaper image © The British Library Board. All rights reserved. With thanks to The British Newspaper Archive (www.britishnewspaperarchive.co.uk).

— or sometimes complete programmes of films — and then, in July 1909, The Southend-on-Sea Theatre Co., became the new proprietors and changed the theatre's name to the 'New Hippodrome.'

Later in 1909, the New Hippodrome began to present, by popular request, Sunday concerts by military and other, bands. These included the Band of the Royal Artillery School of Gunnery in July, followed by the Grenadier Guards Band who gave two performances in the October. Later years also saw concerts by H.M. Royal Engineers string band, the orchestral band of H. M. Royal Marines, the 5th Battalion, Rifle Brigade, the Royal Naval Air Service Training

Establishment, the Sheerness Military Band, and the Royal Garrison Artillery Band. Outside of the military, the Highgate United Silver Prize Band and Sheerness Boy's Silver Band were said to receive enthusiastic welcomes in the 1920s.

Management by the Southend-on-Sea Theatre Co., didn't seem to last long. In April 1910, Mr. Barnet Pareezer, the proprietor of theatres in Lowestoft, King's Lynn and Southend took over the lease of the Hippodrome. He was said to have gained golden opinions wherever he catered for the amusement of the public. He explained that rather than offering an arrangement at one theatre, he could offer artistes a week at each of his five theatres, therefore bringing new and better known performers to Sheerness. The name of the theatre was changed back from the New Hippodrome to the Hippodrome only.

The new proprietor was true to his word in bringing well-known and exciting dramatic and variety performances to the Hippodrome, some of them being particular unusual, even

The Hippodrome,
SHEERNESS

Lessee.. .. .. .. PAREEZER.
Resident Manager.. HENRY DANSON

SATURDAY, MARCH 9th,

LAST NIGHT of
"IT'S ALWAYS THE WOMAN."

MONDAY, Mar. 11th,
and During the Week.

'BABES IN THE WOOD.'

MATINEE—SATURDAY, March 16th—2.30.

Prices, 4d., 6d., 1'-, 1/6, 2'-, 2/6.

LATE TRAIN Every Wednesday and Saturday to Faversham, Sittingbourne, & Queenborough, leaving Sheerness Dockyard Station at 11.15 p.m.

Sheerness Times and General Advertiser. Saturday March 9th 2012. Newspaper image © The British Library Board. All rights reserved. With thanks to The British Newspaper Archive (www.britishnewspaperarchive.co.uk).

sensational. In April 1912, the hippodrome was crowded to see the wonderful electrical and hypnotic waves of Dr. Walford Bodie, described as the renowned bloodless surgeon. Using his powers of hypnotism he put members of the audience under his influence. He also conducted weird electrical experiments with the assistance of medium La Belle Electra, who was put into a trance. This was followed by demonstrating to the audience how criminals were electrocuted in Sing-Sing Prison, New York. He then undertook various other dangerous experiments.

Pantomime again held sway at the Hippodrome in March 1912, when Messrs. Robert Adams and Charles Kay presented their company in a gorgeous production of "Babes in the Wood." Plenty of fun was introduced, for which a cast of comedians had been engaged, including Mr. Charles Kay (from the "Palace," London) as the Baron; Mr. Bert Morland as the Dame, Mr. Leslie Harold as the Page, and Messrs. Mea and Him as the robbers. The last named were the delight of children, who never failed to appreciate the comic duet. The entire production was carried by the company, including special scenery, dresses, and all effects, plus a specially augmented orchestra. Charles Kay introduced a new patriotic song, written, composed, and sung by himself.

In May 1913 an element of the countryside was brought to the Hippodrome, when Jack Daw, the bird imitator appeared at the theatre. Coming on to the stage dressed as a tramp, he entertained his audience in many different bird dialects, from the carol of the skylark to the high-pitched and unassuming twitter of the robin and the anxious clucking of a young chick. His imitation of the last-named, as he chased an imaginary one round the stage, was exceedingly amusing. So realistic was it 'that one could almost see the imaginary chick. Not quite, though.'

In another change of name in December 1914, the Hippodrome began to be promoted and referred to in advertisements and in press reports as the Sheerness Hippodrome Theatre. This was then shortened to just 'Hippodrome Theatre' during 1915.

The ability of the Hippodrome to bring in some of the country's biggest stars was highlighted in February 1915 when Marie Lloyd, the ever popular queen of comedy, appeared in front of crowded houses for twice-nightly performances for five nights. So much so that at the end of her performance on the first night she had to repeatedly bow in acknowledgements of the hearty response, and receiving a gift of a handsome bouquet. The *Sheerness Times Guardian* of the 20th February 1915 commented

Advertisement in the Sheerness Times Guardian for Marie Lloyd's appearance at the Sheerness Hippodrome Theatre. Newspaper image © The British Library Board. All rights reserved. With thanks to The British Newspaper Archive (www.britishnewspaperarchive.co.uk).

that 'the charm of her pleasing personality, her graceful dancing, and the arts and wiles of her distinctive impersonations all contribute to an effect that makes for the success that has undoubtedly placed her in the forefront of her profession.'

Just a few months later a feature of the programme at the Hippodrome that received appreciative applause was the impersonation of Charlie Chaplin by one of the Four Delvines in their original musical comedy act. However, what really brought the house down was that of Rochefort, who performed on a one-string fiddle, making it sing, whistle and mimic, ending with an item which appeared to be almost impossible on a one-stringed instrument.

Such had been the interest in the Charlie Chaplin impersonation by the Delvines that the Hippodrome presented its own Charlie Chaplin competition in September 1915, commencing on the Monday evening and continuing nightly until each evenings' winners came together for the second performance on Friday night for the grand final. The judges throughout the week were the audience; the entrant receiving the greatest amount of applause at each house being selected for the final. All the entrants were said to be particularly good. The prize for the best impersonation and mannerisms was £2. 2s.

The Hippodrome continued with its successful programmes of drama, variety, opera, concerts and films during the remainder of the second decade of the 1920s, with the Sheerness Times Guardian in September 1922 noting that 'the standard of films exhibited at the Hippodrome has never stood higher than it does now, and in conjunction with the excellent Hippodrome orchestra and luxurious surroundings, it is not difficult to understand why this imposing

*An early photograph of the Hippodrome buildings
on the corner of the Broadway.
Illustration by kind permission of Trevor Edwards.*

house of entertainment stands an easy first in the estimation of the Sheerness public.'

By 1924 the Hippodrome was placing advertisements in local papers under the name of the Hippodrome Cinema, although for drama, variety or when interspersed with concert performances, the advertising was still only placed as the Hippodrome. This seemed to be the pattern of management through the remainder of the 1920s and much of the 1930s.

EXTENSIVE IMPROVEMENTS AND THE ONSET OF WAR

Then in February 1939 the Hippodrome closed for extensive improvements, including the complete redecoration, drastic improvements to the heating and ventilation, a new screen, and the whole of the ground floor being re-seated and re-carpeted, together with a complete transformation of the vestibule. A considerable amount of outdoor repairs were also to be effected. Once completed it was expected that 'the Hippodrome would become the comfiest cinema in Sheerness.

It was also teased that the entertainment that was to be offered in the refurbished Hippodrome would include the greatest array of pictures that had ever been booked at a cinema in Sheerness, as well an announcement about a matter that would be of wide interest to the entertainment public in Sheerness. It was then later announced that a first-class London company had been engaged and the theatre would be changing over to "live" entertainment when it re-opened. Repertory had a large following in Sheerness and the opportunity to see and hear live plays and variety would be greatly welcomed.

On Easter Monday evening, 1939, The Standard Repertory Company opened at the Hippodrome, with Councillor C F Hanlon, Chairman of the Urban District Council being present to "launch" the show with the blessings of the local authority and the townspeople. The *Sheerness Times Guardian* of the 9th April, 1939, commented that 'these performances will revive former memories, particularly amongst the older members of the society, who will recall the days when plays, musical comedies, and variety filled the bill at this house of entertainment, which has undergone many changes during its existence in the town. From what we hear, this is regarded as a step in the right direction, and it is to be hoped that the enterprise of the Management will be backed up by generous support on the part of the public. '

At the of April 1939, the newly refurbished Hippodrome

introduced its first full variety bill, a real live entertainment without a dull moment from beginning to end. Laughter, music and thrills were all blended in pleasing proportions, and it was certainly a show that should not be missed. Opening with two lively tap dancing girls, followed by a ventriloquial act in which Douglas Leonard earned the admiration of all.

Coming on stage he is seen with two stowaways and a parrot and keeps up a continuous flow of conversation with the stowaways, with frequent interruptions from the bird. Other high spots in the programme included jugglers, a "talk with chalks" by Louis Valentine who gave a bright and breezy talk while executing lightning sketches of various kinds of hats and their wearers. There was also a blind whistler and bird imitator, a magician, comedians and an excellent trio of musicians.

Together with the Standard Repertory Company the Hippodrome theatre continued with is programme of drama, revue and variety during the rest of 1939 and into 1940s until World War II and the Battle of Britain taking place in the skies above Kent and Sheppey brought the theatre to a close. It was then taken over by the Admiralty and used as a storage depot for naval storage, throughout the War

Post War, the Hippodrome was take over and re-opened by Mr. Louis Moms, who then sold it on to the Essoldo Circuit chain in 1947. By the latter part of the 1940s, and now under the management of Essoldo, the Hippodrome once again started to present and show live first-class variety and revue, with a complete change of programme each week. The *Faversham News* of the 19th August 1949 noted that there were cheap railway tickets to Sheerness every weekday evening, where patrons 'could rely on seeing a good show in comfort.'

The Sheerness Hippodrome was also now included in The Stage listing of performers each week at each of the UK's theatres. Some of the repertory, shows and revues noted in The Stage as appearing at the Hippodrome over the coming few years included: "Sons of the Seas" in March 1950, Norman Harper, Eddie Mendoza and Band in May 1950, Mexano and Band and Variety Co. in May 1950, "Nudes are News" with Harry Hollis, Duval Girls, Maureen Comfort, Roberta Dexter, Michel the Clown and Mickey Hayes in September 1950, "Opportunity Knocks" in November 1950, and the pantomime "Snow White" in December 1950.

A second pantomime, "Aladdin," followed in January 1951. Some of the other notable repertory and variety performances in 1952, 1953 and 1954, were by the International Theatre Company who were at the Hippodrome in June 1952, The Keith Salberg Repertory Company in May 1953, and Tom E. Bradley's Summer Show in July 1954. No further listing for the Sheerness Hippodrome appear in *The Stage* after the end of 1954. The Hippodrome finally closed after almost 80 years of variety, music hall, repertory, big bands and concerts in August 1955.

MUSIC HALL AND ASSEMBLY ROOMS OPEN IN WHITSTABLE IN THE 1860S

The opening of a brand new music hall and public entertainment centre in Whitstable took place way back in February 1868. The public on the day were invited for tea at 5 o'clock, followed by a concert and readings. Upwards of thirty performers participated in the opening performances, including seven vocalist and a brass band. Admission, including tea, was set at one shilling.

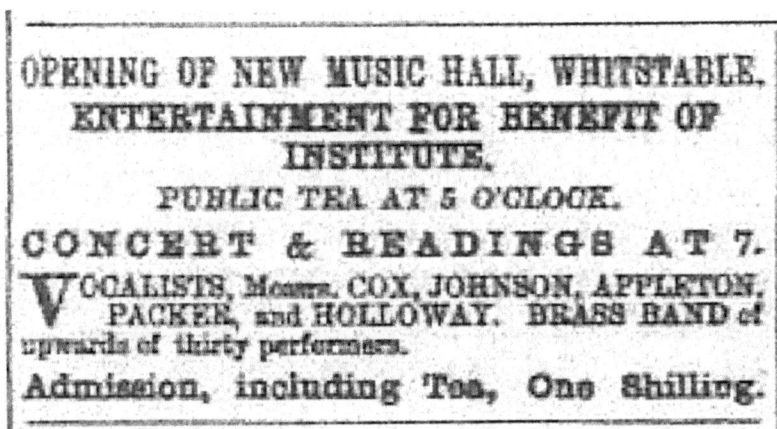

OPENING OF NEW MUSIC HALL, WHITSTABLE,
ENTERTAINMENT FOR BENEFIT OF
INSTITUTE.
PUBLIC TEA AT 5 O'CLOCK.
CONCERT & READINGS AT 7.
VOCALISTS, Messrs. COX, JOHNSON, APPLETON,
PACKER, and HOLLOWAY. BRASS BAND of
upwards of thirty performers.
Admission, including Tea, One Shilling.

Opening of Whitstable's New Music Hall un 1868. Newspaper
image © The British Library Board. All rights reserved.
With thanks to The British Newspaper Archive
(www.britishnewspaperarchive.co.uk).

Thoughts of building a hall in Whitstable that could be used for public purposes had first begun in early 1867, but this did not initially materialize. It was only later in the year that an enterprising townsman, Thomas G. Browning, took the matter into his own hands and decided to erect a spacious two-storey public building at his own risk on a piece of land adjoining Mr. Goldfinch's store in Horse Bridge Road.

The upper floor measuring 60 feet by 30 feet would be for public entertainment; the ground floor would be divided into compartments or rooms and used as accommodation for the Whitstable Oyster Company, The Institute, and an Auction Mart and offices. The building work commenced in October 1867 and was completed in January 1868, ready for the February opening concert.

A couple of months later, in April 1868, another excellent concert, presented by Messrs. Johnson and Cox, was given at Whitstable's 'New Music Hall.' They were assisted by an Emily Spiller from London, Mr. Longhurst of Canterbury, and Messrs. Penn, Johnson junior, Appleton, Packer and Holloway, whose united efforts were said to make a very attractive programme. Miss Spiller was particularly noted as a pleasing vocalist, singing four songs and each time being rapturously encored. The evening was very successful, but the attendance was said to be limited.

By the end of the first year attendances were much more satisfactory, with the well-known and favourite comic, Harry Aldridge, giving a concert at the Music Hall in December 1868, attracting an audience of some 300 persons. He was assisted by Barny Ryan, the Irish delineator (the act of outlining or representing something with words), Dugwar, the Indian juggler, and once again, Messrs. Cox, J. Johnson, F. Johnson, and Packer.

However, low audience numbers at the Music Hall — about 150 persons — were back to the fore in August 1869 when Emma Stanley, an accomplished lady gave a very clever entertainment entitled "The Seven Ages of Woman." It was reported that of all the entertainments undertaken by one person, not one was as complete as the one given by Miss Stanley.

A Grand Concert at the Music Hall on Tuesday 7th September 1869, was announced by Mr. Charles Roberts, The Great Metropolitan Musical Agent, and Caterer to most of the Nobility, Foresters and Odd Fellows, Fetes and Galas. The Concert, with a cast of eminent London artists, included Madame Kollman, Miss Nellie Gelton, vocalist and burlesque actress, Mr. Harry Symonds, comedian, Mr Will Cruikshanks, Ethiopian grotesque, Dugwar the Queen's juggler, The Brothers Vercells, the great Continental and musical clowns, and Mr. C. Westhall.

The following month, a company of artistes styling themselves as the Georgia Minstrels, or 'The Great American Slave Troupe,' entertained with a perfect performance to a crowded audience — of a size seldom seen before — at the Music Hall. The company comprised sixteen performers, the majority of whom were genuine coloured men, who prior to 1865 were said to be held as slaves in the State of Georgia.

A local newspaper report stated 'We have witnessed numerous companies of minstrels, but none in any respect superior to these. An important feature of the entertainment is the singing and acting of a diminutive "darkie," who assumes the name of "Japanese Tommy," whose antics created roars of laughter. Altogether the entertainment was one which could not fail to give satisfaction, and it reflected credit on all who took part in it.'

A feature of entertainment presented regularly at the Music Hall was "Penny Readings," a Victorian tradition popularised by Charles Dickens, in which public performances of readings and musical entertainment were given, with audience members paying only a penny to attend.

In February 1870 for example, a crowded audience assembled at the Hall for the fourth in a series of penny readings. A very pleasing entertainment was afforded through the united exertions of the Rev. H. W. Bateman, the Rev. W. Blissard, and Mr. S. Saunders, as readers, and Mrs and Miss Bateman, Miss Rigden, Messrs. Johnson and Harrison, and the Church Choir, who gave a selection of vocal and instrumental music.

A month later, something rather different was presented to, again, a large company assembled at the Hall for an exhibition of views of the Holy Land and scenes of the Lord's life on earth, supplemented by a display of a number of copies of famous works of art.

On the occasion of a Grand Concert in January 1874 the Music Hall was granted a licence until midnight, just prior to a concert being given by the Canterbury Cavalry Depot Band, assisted by several vocalists, the proceeds in aid of the Soldiers' Daughters' Home. Vocal and instrumental concerts, with profits in aid of various charities and the homeless poor, continued regularly over the next few years.

Variety performances still managed to attract good audiences into the 1880s, such as Vance's Merry Makers in August 1881. Artists appearing for this well-attended show included Miss Eunice Irving, comedienne from the Egyptian Hall; Fred Harrington, a mimic and vocal comedian; Mr. Vivian Blanchard, musical trouvère (the French word for troubadour); and Mr. Albert G. Vance, author, composer and vocal comedian.

It was during the first half of 1881 that the name of the Whitstable

Music Hall changed, to now become the Whitstable Assembly Rooms, and now being used for a wider rage of activities, such as various auctions, all designed to try and attract a greater income. By the spring of 1882, the Assembly Rooms are being additionally used for clothing auctions and bazaars, but with a notice later appearing in the *Whitstable Times and Herne Bay Herald* of 29th July stating that unless the Assembly Rooms were better patronised they would be closed.

Fortunately, audiences again seemed to pick up when Mr. Horace Lennard's Entertainments presented the first a series of dramatic, musical and other entertainments to be held under his direction at the Assembly Rooms in October 1884. Despite severe wet weather, all the reserved seats were filled, and the attendance in other parts of the Rooms was numerous when Mr. Pyatt, the

ROYAL REFINED COMBINATION COMPANY.

ASSEMBLY ROOMS, WHITSTABLE.

Monday, December 2nd, and two following nights.

Special and Expensive Engagement of

DR. HOLDEN,

THE COURT MAGICIAN AND WONDER WORKER

(Engaged direct from the Egyptian Hall, London).

UNDER the patronage of Her Most Gracious Majesty, the Queen-Empress, His Imperial Majesty, Nas'r-ed-Din Shah, King of Kings, their Royal Highnesses, the Prince and Princess of Wales, Etc.,

In his marvellous entertainment, entitled

CHARMATION

(Title Registered.)

Introducing for the first time in this country. Astounding feats of Necromantic Science.

Most Important Engagement of

PROFESSOR HOWLETT'S ROYAL MARIONETTEN THEATRE,

Which has had the distinguished honour of appearing before Her Most Gracious Majesty The Queen, and Their Royal Highnesses The Prince and Princess of Wales, on June 22nd, 1887. (Engaged direct from the Establishment Moisachia, Munich, Germany.) This unique, varied, and highly refined entertainment will introduce some of the most elaborate scenes and sensational novelties that have ever been introduced by marionettes.

Christy Minstrel Troupe.

Marvellous Fantoccini Exploits.

Grand Comic Pantomime.

Dioramic Scenery Effects.

The whole a Triumph of Mechanism and Manipulation.

Successful Engagement of PROFESSOR

VAL MILLER

America's Premier Ventriloquist, with his Comical Figures. Introducing Songs, Jokes, Conundrums, &c.

(Engaged direct from the Empire Theatre).

Startling Engagement of MONSIEUR

LE GARCIAN

THE MARVELLOUS EQUILIBRIST.

Who will introduce all the Latest Novelties in Juggling, Balancing, Plate Manipulation, &c., whilst on a Revolving Globe.

The Whole being the Most Refined, Amusing, and Select Combination of Talent Travelling.

Prices of Admission : 2s., 1s., and 6d. Children half-price to 2s. and 1s. seats.

Doors open at 7.30. Commence at 8 o'clock.

Tickets may be obtained at Mr. Mr. W. J. Cox, High Street.

1889 advertisement. Newspaper image © The British Library Board. All rights reserved. With thanks to The British Newspaper Archive (www.britishnewspaperarchive.co.uk).

well-known London bass from Her Majesty's Opera and Royal Albert Hall concerts, was reported to have been in splendid voice, being rapturously received and each of his songs encored. Mr. Henry Hallam, the tenor from the Alhambra, London, also contributed to the melody of the evening.

The *Whitstable Times and Herne Bay Herald* of 12th January 1889 announced that pantomime would be coming to Whitstable the following week, when three performances of the new popular pantomime "Beauty and the Beast," would be presented at the Assembly Rooms. The editorial commented that 'A pantomimic representation in Whitstable is a novelty, but we are in no doubt that the entertainment will be largely patronised.'

In July 1889, Miss Ida Cecil's MIZPAH Company came to the Assembly Rooms for three nights in arrangement with J. B. Mulholland, Esq., of the Grand Theatre, Nottingham. The entertainment included a full company of London artistes, together with splendid wardrobes, and special scenery that included a great mechanical change.

Astounding feats of necromantic science were promised when it was announced that the special and expensive engagement of Dr. Holden, the 'Court Magician and Wonder Worker,' direct from the Egyptian Hall and under the patronage of Her Most Gracious Majesty, the Queen Empress, His Imperial Majesty, Nas'r-ed Shah, King of KIngs, and their Royal Highnesses, the Prince and Princess of Wales, would be appearing at the Assembly Rooms in December 1889 in his marvellous entertainment, entitled Charmation.

Also announced as a forthcoming important entertainment was

the engagement of Professor Howlett's Royal Marionetten Theatre, which had had the distinguished honour of appearing before Her Most Gracious Majesty The Queen, and Their Royal Highnesses The Prince and Princess of Wales. This unique, varied, and highly refined entertainment introduce some of the most elaborate scenes and sensational novelties that have ever been introduced by marionettes.

The marionettes were to be followed by the successful engagement of Professor Val Miller, America's premier Ventriloquist, with his comical figures, introducing songs, jokes and conundrums, and the starring engagement of Monsieur Le Garcian, the marvellous equilibrist, who introduced all the latest novelties in juggling, balancing and plate manipulation, all whilst balancing on a revolving globe.

It was not always big name or London artistes performing at the Assembly Rooms. Concerts and entertainment were also given by well-know local performers. A Grand Variety Entertainment in February 1891 included locals in "The Bogie Man," a laughable sketch entitled "I'll kill the cat," and the screaming farce "Which shall I marry."

Some of London's leading artists were back at the Assembly Rooms in September 1892, when Mr. Frederic De Lara presented his High Society Entertainment, supported by Miss Evelyn Hughes, the marvellous child actress from the Theatre Royal, Drury Lane, Miss Rhoda Larkin, Miss Kate Cutler, Ms. Watson, Mr. Walter Bridge (also from the Theatre Royal), Mr. Fredk. Conneaux and Miss Sophie Larkin, who presented a programme of miscellaneous entertainment that included "Little Jessie," "A Capital Joke," and "Stage Coach."

ASSEMBLY ROOMS,
WHITSTABLE.

FOR THREE NIGHTS ONLY!!!

September 13th, 14th, and 15th.

PITNEY WESTON'S
DRAMATIC TOURING COMPANY

WILL play on THURSDAY and SATURDAY, SEPTEMBER 13th and 15th, the beautiful Drama

" DEVOTION FOR A LIFE,"

IN FIVE TABLEAUX,

And on FRIDAY, SEPTEMBER 14th,

" LURED TO RUIN,"

IN FIVE ACTS.

Front Seats, 2s. Second Seats, 1s. Gallery and Promenade, 6d.

DOORS OPEN AT 7.30; TO COMMENCE AT 8.

Tickets at Mr. W. J. Cox, High Street, where Plan of Hall may be seen.

1894 advertisement. Newspaper image ©

Pitney Weston's Dramatic Touring Company visited the Assembly Rooms for three nights in September 1894 to present the beautiful drama "Devotion for a LIfe," in five tableaux. "Lured to Ruin" in five acts was presented on the Friday night. Miss Emily Thorne, from Toole's Theatre also appeared each evening.

Following the end of performances at the Theatre and Assembly Rooms at the end of September 1985, they were closed for a week for renovation and the erection of a new proscenium. The work was a great success, the interior of the building being presented as pleasing and attractive, with the numerous audiences for the two re-opening evening performances by Miss Sarah Thorne's Dramatic Company, (From the Theatre Royal, Margate), of Tom Taylor's famous drama "The Ticket of Leave Man," and Jerome K. Jerome's successful play "Woodharrow Farm."

THEATRE & ASSEMBLY ROOMS,
WHITSTABLE-ON-SEA.
Messrs. John Wright and Co., Limited,
BIRMINGHAM AND LONDON,

In co-operation with the Gas Company, Whitstable,
HAVE ARRANGED AN
EXHIBITION
OF
Gas Cooking and Heating Appliances,
COMBINED WITH A SERIES OF
High-Class Lectures on Cookery,
IN THE ABOVE HALL.

Tuesday, April 6th to Friday, April 9th (inclusive).

Demonstrations twice daily, at 3.0 and 7.30 p.m., by Miss ADA BALL,
Gold Medalist, South Kensington School of Cookery.

The Enamelled Steel-Lined "Eureka" Cooker, winner of 60 Highest
Awards, may be seen in action, and may be hired at the Exhibition.

Interesting Local Exhibits.
Music at Intervals.
ADMISSION FREE.

*1897 advertisement. Newspaper image © The British Library
Board. All rights reserved. With thanks to The British Newspaper
Archive (www.britishnewspaperarchive.co.uk).*

No little gratification for the works were expressed by the audience, which were said to have been carried out at considerable cost. The performances were highly appreciated, the pleasure being enhanced, in no small measure, by the excellent incidental music performed by an efficient band under the direction of Mr. Hemsley.

Something rather different took place at the Assembly Rooms in April 1897, when Messrs. John Wright and Co. Limited, in co-operation with the Whitstable Gas Company, arranged an exhibition of gas cooking and heating appliances, which was combined with demonstrations of appliances twice daily, together with a series of high-class lectures on cookery and music during the intervals.

The showing of animated films at the Assembly Rooms was also a regular entertainment. In August 1897, animated photographs of the Queen's Diamond Jubilee Procession were presented. Said to be faithfully reproduced, and with all the movements of real life by the Cinematograph. Life-like moving photographs of the Queen, and thirty-five entertainers, were said to be most interesting.

Another cinematograph evening took place in April 1898 when, under the Wesleyan auspices, animated pictures included a London fire, a railway scene, diving from a pier head, negroes diving, and a 'sleepy coachman.' There was also an exhibition of splendid lantern slides. During the evening the Whitstable Mandolin Band played selections which were much appreciated

In April 1898 the audience at the Assembly Rooms was delighted with selections of music by the Whitstable String Band, who were loudly encored. Amongst the performers, Mr. Sparshott's song was very ably rendered, and Mr. Snell was very highly applauded for his comic song, following this with an encore for his "Oompah" song.

Said to be the great 'Success of the Century,' Mr. W. S. Penly's Company from the Globe Theatre brought "Charley's Aunt" to the Assembly Rooms in September 1898. The *Whitstable Times and Herne Bay Herald*, Saturday 16 April, 1898, reported that 'It is almost needless to say anything with regard to this amusing comedy, because it is undoubtedly the success of the century. We strongly advise those who want a hearty laugh not to miss the opportunity of seeing the little lady from Brazil where the nuts come from.'

In June 1899 the Whitstable Theatre and Assembly Rooms were

sold by auction. The promotional auction advertisement stated that the building was substantially built of brick, with an iron roof, and that there was an adjoining brick-built dwelling house adjoining, currently in the occupation of Mr. H. Browning. There was also a yard at the rear. The whole property had a frontage to Horsebridge Road of about 50 feet, and to the Middle Wall of about 54 feet. The house, offices and part of the yard attracted an aggregate rental of £50 per year.

Two months later, it was announced that the Assembly Rooms had been renovated and decorated throughout and now presented a bright appearance, ready for performances during the rest of the ensuing season. The reopening Bohemian Concert attracted a large audience and everyone enjoyed an excellent programme. Some first class theatrical companies were said to be giving performances in the course of the winter months.

Cinematograph pictures continued to be presented at the beginning of a new century of entertainment. An animated picture concert in December 1900, using the very latest non-flickering cinematograph, was used to show the Boer War, including the departure of troops and the hoisting of the British Flag at Pretoria, as well as scenes from the War in China.

The brightest musical show on tour came to the Assembly Rooms in September 1907 when a first-class company of London artists presented "Such a Nice Girl." A show that included catchy songs, new dances, and claimed to be funnier than any pantomime.

The September 26th, 1908, edition of The *Whitstable Times and Herne Bay Herald* reported that the comedian, Charles Kay, was part of a Grand Concert at the Assembly Rooms and that audiences never tired of his original humour. The Concert was put together with three of the artists who had also achieved much success in Whitstable and Herne Bay, together with the assistance of Miss Aubrey Hylton, solo pianist from the Royal Albert and Bechstein Halls. Miss Hedda Hirleman acted as the general director and producer for the evening.

During the Concert Charles Kay sang 'The Beautiful Tale of Love' and when encored gave the audience 'Girls, Girls, Beautiful Girls'. Also on the programme was Hedda Hirleman who sang 'Pussy had another sardine' at the piano and then rendered a duet with Charles Kay entitled 'Nobody knows, nobody cares'. Both songs were encored. His final song was 'Come and have a drink with me'

Something different again was advertised at the Assembly Rooms as commencing in January 1910, with the introduction of roller skating sessions that would be available whenever the hall was not engaged for other purposes.

An advertisement in August 1910 now promoted The Whitstable Electric Picture Company, which would be showing films at the Assembly Rooms — the most comfortable Hall in Whitstable — every evening. These would include Tragedy, Comedy, Drama, Comic, Scenic and Topical events.

Moving to July 1914, and Mr Hare, the popular London comedian presented his Loudon West End Company in "The Mollusc," which had twice been honoured by visits from the late King Edward, and subsequently the present King at the Criterion Theatre, London. In a newspaper announcement it was explained that 'A Mollusc is an animal of the sea, which clings to a rock, and lets the tide flow over its head. Apply this to the laciest of lacy people, and you have Mrs. Baxter! Then think what a rotten time poor Baxter must have of it. And there's a most pretty governess looking after the Baxter's offspring. Fancy Mrs. Baxter having the energy to supply an offspring (two in fact!). Baxter falls in love with the Mollusc and his wife becomes jealous. How is she stopped?'

Little in the way of touring variety and drama shows appears to have taken place at the Assembly Rooms during the 1914 - 1918 War years. Activity was more likely to be found with Recruitment Meetings, such as that given by Mr. John Hunt, F.R.C.I. who gave a talk about Germany, the lead-up to the War and followed this with a lantern slide lecture of photographs taken at the war. October 1915 provided another interest when A. Seddon, of the Manchester Regiment and a well-known boxer, gave a boxing exhibition at the hall on Monday 1st November.

Following the ending of the War, a meeting of the Whitstable Shops Committee was held at the Assembly Rooms in late October 1918. This was to resolve to support the further appeal to the Home Secretary to be made by the Early Closing Association in favour of compulsory closing shops 7 o'clock. It was said that the majority of shopkeepers in Whitstable already closed at 6 o'clock four days week, at 1 o'clock on Wednesday, and 8 o'clock on Saturday.

Newly re-decorated once again, the Assembly Rooms re-opened in April 1920 for the fist performance of a clever one-act play entitled "The Show-Down," described as an episode in one act and written by Bijou Primrose-Pechey and Valentine. It was said to be a splendid production, well-acted and well-received and forecast to have a big

ASSEMBLY ROOMS,
WHITSTABLE.

Three Nights Only,
Monday, Tuesday, Wednesday,
Jan. 17th, 18th & 19th.

Enormous Attraction
JIMMY WOOD
presents his
Grand Screamingly Funny
Christmas Pantomime

Robinson Crusoe

And the King of the Cannibal
Islands.
In ten charming scenes.
And an Old-fashioned
HARLEQUINADE
Introducing the usual
Clowns and Pantaloons.

Doors open each evening at 7.30.
Commence at 8.
Early Doors open at 7.

Prices of Admission.
3/-,   2/4,   1/3.
(Including Entertainment Tax).
Seats can be booked at Ridout's
Library, Harbour Street.

Robinson Crusoe advertisement. Source:
The Whitstable Times and Tankerton
Press. January 18 1921

run when staged in London

The Whitstable Amateur Operatic and Dramatic Society were active in the early 1920s and presented Gilbert and Sullivan's dramatic cantata "Trial by Jury" in mid-April, followed a few weeks later by a whist drive and dance at the Assembly Rooms, with an attendance of about 80. The same month saw the Whitstable Lawn Tennis Club invited members and anyone interested in tennis to attend at meeting at the hall, as well as a whist drive by the Whitstable Women Voters' League. In August the Whitstable Annual Regatta and Carnival Fancy Dress Dance was held at the Assembly Rooms.

At the end of October 1920, Messrs. Cornwall Jolliffe and W. Scott-Gordon announced that they would be making every effort to present weekly high-class theatrical and musical attractions at the Assembly Rooms and the favour of Whitstable's esteemed patronage was solicited. Their very first programme was "The Vivacities," said to be everything that is new in song, dance and burlesque and a riot of laughter.

By January 1921, the Assembly Rooms were once presenting variety concerts — and now pantomime. At that time, Mr. Jimmy Wood and his company of pantomime comedians payed a visit to the Whitstable Assembly Rooms in their screamingly funny Christmas pantomime "Robinson. Crusoe," written and arranged in ten scenes and concluding with the children's delight, a real old-fashioned harlequinade introducing the usual clowns and pantoloons. '''

Mr. Jimmy Wood, who played Dame Crusoe, and Miss Netta Conroy, who played the title role, were supported by Miss Joan Dan as Polly Perkins, The Scala Quartette Dancers, a full chorus and specialities by Stylo, the great balancing marvel, the Lillian Troup of Barrel Jumpers, Mollie Verell, the famous dancer, and the Two Earles, comedy jugglers, who completed the programme.

The pantomime was followed at the end of January by a staging of "Liberty Hall" by the Whitstable Operatic and Dramatic Society, with takings, after Society expenses, going to the Whitstable Cottage Hospital.

In April 1921 the Assembly Rooms presented for two evenings, Roeckel's Operetta, "The Hours," followed by Louis N. Parker's Play "The Man in the Street." Proceeds from this concert were given to the Whitstable Hockey Club and Whitstable Girl's Choir.

During the 1920's, with the slow decline of touring stage plays and variety acts, there seemed to be less and less promotion of variety entertainment at the Assembly Rooms in favour of more local meetings and activities.

Perhaps because of this and a lower financial return, the Assembly Rooms were again put up for sale by auction on April 15th 1936 and then, in March 1937, the Whitstable Urban District Council, Town Planning Committee, reported that consideration was been given to the question of the acquisition of a site suitable for the erection of a branch library, and information had been received that the Assembly Rooms, Horsebridge Road, Whitstable, could be acquired at a favourable figure, It was recommended that the District Valuer be requested to negotiate with the owner of the Assembly Rooms, Horsebridge Road, Whitstable, in connection with the possible acquisition of the property by the Council for the purposes of a library. Nothing appeared to come from this proposal.

In October 1938 the Assembly Rooms announced that there would be a whist drive every Monday and Friday at 8pm, followed by dancing every Saturday evening from 8pm to 11pm, commencing Saturday, October 22nd. The Newspaper advertising for the evenings added, 'Bus stops at the door.' Dancing and whist drives continued in 1939.

Whitstable Football Club's Grand New Year's Carnival Dance took place at the Assembly Rooms on Monday 2nd January 1939, with music to the Rythym Boy's Dance Band.

By December 1939, the Saturday evening dances were being run at The Assembly Rooms by Chestfield Radio, with music by George Dunn and His Band. One other difference, there was now a cafe on the premises.

In 1940, during almost continuous daily air-raids the building suffered some damage from bombs dropped on the town by German bombers. The building was later restored and during the 1950's and into the 1960s, it was used for hosting some pop concerts and dances, as well as being used by the Whitstable Old Time Dance Club.

In November 1965 the popular local group, the Commuters, who had made a disc at the L.B.C. Recording Studios at the end of July for a London recording company, played at a dance at the Assembly Rooms.

A supermarket, after various planning applications for warehouses, multiple stores, and a supermarket, as well as appeals all going back to at least 1960, was approved by the Council in 1963 and eventually created in the lower level, with the entertainments moved upstairs. By the mid 1960s the upper room, now under new management, was being regularly used for Bingo. In 1987 it was in use as a community support centre. It was demolished and the Horsebridge Arts & Entertainments centre was then built on the site. This opened in 2004.

NEW ENTERTAINMENT VENUE IN A POPULAR NORTH KENT COASTAL RESORT

While there were a number of music hall and variety theatres already well established in many of Kent's coastal towns from around the 1870s and 1880s, there was still apparently room for new, and often smaller, venues to become established, become popular and able to attract a regular audience in the early 1900s, such as the New Pavilion, later known as The Lawn, in Tankerton, or even venues such as the Seasalter Parish Hall.

The concert and variety venue that first became known as the New Pavilion, started its life when a Mr. and Mrs. Parker purchased land on both sides of Tankerton Road, to the east of Whitstable, in 1901, and applied for planning permission to build a hotel. Even before the building was completed they had already applied (in July 1902) for a liquor licence for the soon to be completed Tankerton Hotel. They also fenced off the area of land they had purchased on the Tankerton slopes opposite where the hotel was being constructed.

The Tankerton Hotel opened for business in June 1903, offering accommodation and meeting

CLIFF CONCERTS
(OPPOSITE TANKERTON HOTEL).

On Saturday Next,
AUGUST 27TH, AT 8 OCLOCK,

THE DOMINOES
Will give a GRAND

COMPLIMENTARY CONCERT
TO

MR. HICKMAN SMITH.
SPECIAL ITEMS !

Souvenir Programmes will be on Sale.
Limited number of Reserved Seats, 1s. Other Seats, 6d.
Seats may now be Reserved at RIDOUT'S LIBRARY, Harbour Street.

Whitstable Times and Herne Bay Herald. Saturday 27th August 1904. Newspaper image © The British Library Board. All rights reserved. With thanks to The British Newspaper Archive (www.britishnewspaperarchive.co.uk).

175

rooms, arranging dinners and dances, a smoking room, and some entertainment. By the end of June, the "Dominoes" under the direction of Mr. Frank Speaight, commenced a series of complimentary Grand al fresco Cliff Concerts in an open-air stage and pavilion erected on the fenced-off slopes facing the Tankerton Hotel.

In previous years, The Dominoes advertised their Cliff Concerts as being near the Tower Gardens and, then, from 1901 at Tankerton Cliff. These Complimentary Concerts, now regularly held on the slopes opposite the Tankerton Hotel, continued through 1903 and on into 1904. Now organised by Mr. Horace Royle's concert party, the variety concerts continued to extend with large audiences to be found at the pavilion each evening. Sacred concerts were also given on Sunday evenings and were thoroughly appreciated by the audience.

By the summer of 1905 Horace Royle's famous concert party had taken up its quarters in a pretty little new single-story utilitarian building, and now called the New Pavilion, which had been constructed on the sloping Cliff Concert site opposite the Tankerton Hotel, attracting large and enthusiastic audiences, who were reported to thoroughly enjoy the truly admirable entertainment.

Now with a permanent base in the New Pavilion, the Royle Concert Party were able to become more adventurous in their entertainment programmes. A special charity concert by them at the New Pavilion in August 1905 attracted such a large audience that not enough seating could be found, even after commandeering seats from the Tankerton Hotel, the beach, the local Pierrot Concert Party, and various nearby homes.

The artistes for the concert were said to be in exceptional form, with singers, comedians, an impersonator, a ventriloquist and a series of truly erie "living pictures," including reproductions of famous paintings being splendidly portrayed, among the most successful being 'The Duchess of Devonshire' (Gainsborough) and 'The Courtier' (Whistler).

REFINED AND HIGH-CLASS MUSICAL CONCERTS

Concerts at the New Pavilion continued through 1906, 1907 and into the summer of 1908, but by now being successfully run by Mr. Jack Rowlands. This change to Jack Rowlands was first announced in March 1908, with the *Whitstable Times and Herald* of Saturday 7th March, writing that 'a local gentleman who desired to remain anonymous has leased the New Pavilion at Tankerton with a view to supplying a refined and high-class musical party for the season, the entire management of which has been handed over to Mr. Jack Sales (professionally known as Jack Rowlands), a talented young actor, late of the Apollo Theatre, London, and the very successful stage manager of the Whitstable Dramatic Club.

'The concerts will be given for one week at Whitsun, starting on Saturday, June 6th, and the season proper will open on or about July 6th. With a change of programme each week visitors and residents alike will have nothing to complain of in the way of entertainment this season.'

The programme at New Pavilion at the very beginning of August 1908, included Charles Kay. Large houses were said to be the order at this popular resort where it was reported in the *Whitstable Times and Herald* of Saturday 8th August, that in the previous week 'Charles Kay, the topical talker was, if possible, more popular than ever. His parody on the "Old Apple Tree" is screamingly funny and his references to Tankerton's Architecture, Dorando, and the Slevier Case create quite a furore. An excellent portrait of him appeared in last week's *Throne and Country*. Mr. Rowland has wisely re-engaged him to return in September when he will be given a complimentary benefit.'

Then, on August 5th 1908, the New Pavilion was almost completely wrecked by a severe gale. The *Whitstable Times and Herne Bay Herald* of Saturday 8th August, 1908, also reported that 'when daylight broke, Mr. Jack Rowlands was summoned by phone and on his arrival found the whole of the structure completely demolished and the dresses and scenery completely ruined. The gas brackets were bent and in some cases broken off and the windows blown in by the violence of the wind which, owing to the exposed position of the building, was felt in its full force.'

By the end of September, 1908, The Royle Concert Party was again performing at the now already up and running fully repaired New Pavilion, with the concerts as popular as ever. Charles Kay, who had already appeared a number of times in Whitstable, notably at the Assembly Rooms, had a benefit night at the New Pavilion during the week, when there was said to be an excellent house. Jack Rowlands gave some clever renderings of Maurice Chevalier songs, while Miss Edith Earle's charming songs secured her an encore at each appearance and Miss Hedda Hirlemann added further popularity with her song 'Domino.'

July 1909 sees "The White Coons" commence their season at the

New Pavilion, and now under the same management as the Cosy Corner, Whitstable, by arrangement with Mr. W. Kirby, the popular landlord of the Tankerton Hotel. This was followed later in the season by The Mascots, who gave an end of season farewell performance on Saturday, September the 11th.

Something new, novel and original was featured in August 1910 when the famous humorist, Mr. Walter Macnamara (from the Palace, Coliseum, Tivoli and Oxford theatres), presented his travelogues, monologues and burlesque, all supported by a West End company arranged through The General Attractions Bureau.

The Mascots, promoted as a clever troupe of refined entertainers, were back once again, performing three times daily, at the New

The Whitstable Times and Herne Bay Herald. Saturday, July 22nd, 1911. Newspaper image © The British Library Board. All rights reserved. With thanks to The British Newspaper Archive (www.britishnewspaperarchive.co.uk).

Pavilion for the whole summer season commencing in July, 1911, with the theatre now under the management of Mr. Jack Mavis — who claimed he personally selected each artiste. The show continued right through to the end of September.

It was in July 1912 that a brand new summer season show for the New Pavilion under the direction of Messrs. J Rowland Sales and Company was advertised as being finalised and would be announced shortly in the local papers. No mention of a new show, or Messrs. Rowland Sales and Company however, appeared in any papers during the rest of 1912. Nor were there any mentions in any press of any concerts or shows at the New Pavilion during 1912.

THE JOLLITY BOYS OPEN AT THE LAWN

The next announcement came in July 1913, with the *Whitstable Times and Herne Bay Herald*, of Saturday 5 July, 1913, reporting that 'Whitstable people will learn with pleasure that the famous "Jollity Boys," with their red coats and white trousers, and who have

---

THE LAWN, TANKERTON.
Mr. Arthur Vernon's Concert Party,
THE JOLLITY BOYS.

Two Performances Daily at 3 and 8.

Sunday Evening Concerts at 8.15.

A cheque for **10/6** will be given away at every Friday evening performance.

Prices of admission — **6d.** and **3d.**, Reserved **1/-**.

Afternoon Performances — Chairs **2d.**

Whitstable Times and Herne Bay Herald. Saturday 5th July 1913.
Newspaper image © The British Library Board. All rights
reserved. With thanks to The British Newspaper Archive
(www.britishnewspaperarchive.co.uk).

been appearing at Herne Bay for the past twelve years, will transfer their attentions to Whitstable's Tankerton Slopes this season and that they will open at 'The Lawn,' Tankerton, on Monday evening next. The artists include Mr. Arthur Vernon (tenor), Mr. Nigel Effingham (character humorist), Mr. William Henry (bass-baritone), Mr. Barrett Clifton (solo pianist and accompanist). Mr, Fred Rick (light comedian), and Mr. Christopher Easthope (vocalist), and the popular comedian Mr. Charlie Howard.

The New Pavilion, Tankerton, had now been renamed as 'The Lawn,' with the Jollity Boys soon attracting large audiences with their varied and high-class programme.

Mr. Arthur Vernon's company which is eight in number, and each a talented artiste and capable of giving a "turn" that would please the most exacting. The concert items run with a rare swing, and are cleverly worked out. Most of them are extremely comical, while others, not less clever, are in lighter vein.

The Tankerton Hotel and, on the right of the road, t
he original Lawn Pavilion

At about the same time, in July 1913, it was announced that an awning had been erected over site and at the north end, providing a vast improvement and enabling the audience to sit in comfort and sheltered from the rain and the north wind. It was stated that the awning was to be continued round the east side and would result in further added comfort.

Throughout the season, the Jollity Boys enjoyed large audiences and were said to be increasingly drawing their old Herne Bay followers to Whitstable and The Lawn concerts and variety shows. Then, towards the end of the season in September, they introduced Saturday evening singing competitions for ladies and gentlemen to enter; the winners to receive a money prize. This was followed a few weeks later by prizes for children singing, dancing and recitation every Monday, Wednesday and Friday afternoon.

The Jollity Boys were back at The Lawn again for the 1914 summer season commencing at the beginning of July, and achieving large audiences for every performance as their reputation as a refined, clever and most entertaining concert party continued to be enhanced. Performances were said to be most amusing and delightful. Remember, this was all taking place at a time when the country was engaged in the biggest war in the world's history.

SUCCESSFUL SUMMER SEASON DESPITE ANOTHER WAR

The following month, the Admiralty a issued statement that visitors to the seaside towns need have no fear, and they were glad to see that visitors were returning to the seaside in large numbers. This was after a good many visitors had been scared out of Whitstable after the explosion at the Gun Cotton Works the previous week. With the publication of the Admiralty notice greater confidence was being restored and it was anticipated that the town should benefit largely from holiday makers from London now. Indeed, it was already so benefiting the crowds that daily visit The Lawn.

At the end of a most successful 1914 season, concluding in late September, the Jollity Boys announced they would be moving to the Theatre Royal, Canterbury for a few days where it was expected that the good name they had made for themselves in Tankerton would be sure to follow them to the Cathedral city where, there is no doubt, they will receive a welcome no less cordial than that which they had from Whitstable audiences. 'Notwithstanding the European war and the ill-effects it had upon business and also upon pleasure, the Jollity Boys have had a really good season, the patronage extended to them being far in advance of that of last year.'

Despite the ongoing war, Mr. Arthur Vernon's Concert Party were back performing at The Lawn — with the seating area now enclosed in a large and spacious marquee — in July 1915 for the coming, and their third, summer season. However, advertisements now contained the message 'The presence of a lady member to make up our full strength means we have dropped the original title of the Jollity Boys and we are know now as Mr. Arthur Vernon's Concert Party.' There was also a footnote: 'All members of the Jollity Boys performing this season are not eligible for the Army.' Inserted into all promotion was the message ' Soldiers in Uniform half price. Wounded soldiers free.'

In spite of the wartime lighting restrictions at The Lawn the spacious marquee was said to be filled to capacity every evening, with

183

it being universally acknowledged that Mr. Arthur Vernon's Concert Party were giving the public even better programmes than in the past.

There was no ongoing summer season at The Lawn during 1916, 1917 and 1918. Most of the artists that made-up the Jollity Boys and Mr. Vernon's Concert Party in the previous years were now working for the Y. M.C.A. and N.A.C.B, touring the various armed forces camps throughout Great Britain, although they did manage to put a group together to give an occasional concert at the Lawn during this period. The Y.M.C.A., The Entente Costume Concert Party, the Orpheus Concert Party from Canterbury, Miss Lena Ashwell's Concert Party, and various other concert groups provided some entertainment over these three years. It was April 1919 before regular summer season concerts and variety returned to The Lawn with, once again the Jollity Boys — but now reformed with lady members and called the "Jollitees" — performing twice daily with their usual concert items, some burlesque, and good vocal quartets.

Flights from 5/-

Don't miss a Flight in the latest National Flying Services SALOON AIR TAXI at SWALECLIFFE Herne Bay-Whitstable Road. FLYING DAILY

Air taxi service from Swalecliffe in 1930. Reproduced by permission. The Whitstable Times and Tankerton Press. August 30th, 1930.

The *Whitstable Times and Herne Bay Herald* of the 17th May, 1919, wrote 'that with the bathing huts back again on the Tankerton front, provision for teas and refreshments at the new refreshment room near the bandstand, the return of the Jollitees to the Lawn, and aeroplane joy rides along the coast, there ought to be attractions for everybody who visits the town.

The Jollitees again opened for the summer season at The Lawn in 1920 but, at the end of another successful season on the Tankerton Slopes, presented their Grand Farewell Concert on Saturday 25th September. This was then followed for the 1921 and 1922 seasons by Charlie Howard's Concert Party.

Charlie Howard was of course the popular comedian for many years with the Jollity Boys and then the Jollitees. The audiences for his bright and musical shows over the two years were said to be 'larger than has ever been known before.' The members of the company were for the most part new to Tankerton. All of them were said to be excellent, but two of the vocalists stood out for talent far and away above that seen in concert party artistes.'

A change of variety enter-tainment for the 1923 season sees the brand new Lawn Concert Party, under the personal direction of Fred Wilmott, coming to the Tankerton Slopes.

From the 1924 season right

THE LAWN, TANKERTON.

Lessee   -   ·   ·   -   Mrs. Willie Rouse.

Nightly at 8 o'clock.   Doors open 7.30 p.m.

MRS. WILLIE ROUSE presents

THE 1930 BOHEMIANS

Under direction of Mr. BROMLEY CARTER.

ARTISTES :—

Miss Dorothy Gadsden, Soprano.
Mr. Richard Harris, Tenor,
Miss Rene Turner, Soubrette and Dancer,
Miss Nora Drake, Pianiste and Entertainer,
Mr. Tom A. Keele, Light Comedian and Dancer,
and Mr. Bromley Carter, Entertainer.

Booking Office at the Lawn Daily—Mr. Geo. Fox, and Messrs. George Fitts Motors Ltd., Music Lounge, Tankerton Circus. Phone 447—448.

Prices: 2/4 and 1/10 numbered and reserved.
1/3 and 8d., unreserved.
All Prices include Tax.

The Bohemians provided the summer season at The Lawn from 1930 to 1933. Reproduced by permission. The Whitstable Times and Tankerton Press. August 30th, 1930.

185

through the rest of the 1920s decade, and then for the 1931 season, the popular entertainment at The Lawn was provided by 'Wireless' Willie Rouse and his Herne Bay company of the Bohemians and their high-class entertainment of humour, music, and dancing, with each of the artists scoring greatly and being accorded vociferous applause. The *Whitstable Times and Herne Bar Herald* of Saturday 8th August, 1931 noted that 'Having heard Willie Rouse on the wireless is good, but to see him live at the piano is better.' The motto of the Bohemians was promoted as ' To be happy and gay and drive dull care away.'

1932 and 1933 summer seasons at The Lawn were presented by Clay Thomas and Stewart Goss Products. The Lessee was now shown as Mrs. Willie Rouse. The entertainment provided over the two years was promoted as 'Clay Thomas and the Seamews.'

In a Herne Bay court case in November 1933, a former entertainments manager at The Lawn, Albert Edward Wraight, was summoned for issuing tickets for admission to shows at The Lawn without them bearing tax stamps. He was fined £2 for each of two cases, with £3 costs.

A comedy, song and dance show entitled the 'Six of Us,' was the 1934 season's entertainment by Clarkson Rose Productions. The following year saw a number of weeks of 'Living Marionette' performances.

REGULAR REPERTORY DRAMA AND COMEDY PLAYS

by the mid 1930s, The Lawn was not only providing concert shows, but was also now regularly bringing-in repertory companies for weekly drama or comedy plays. These included the Owen Dove

Players with 'The Ghost Train,' in 1937 followed by The Citizen Players in Repertory Company. 'Love on the Dole' ran for several weeks in 1938.

'Les Dominos Noirs,' a Concert Party of Distinction and presented by Miss Nora Webber, came to The Lawn for the 1939 summer season. By the autumn of that year War had been declared and before long the Battle of Britain and air raids over Kent had commenced. The Lawn was now closed and there were no concerts, plays or entertainments promoted for the next six years.

Repertory returned to The Lawn in October 1947, with the Frances Yates London Repertory Company presenting 'Murder Without Crime,' There's Always Juliet' and 'They Walk Alone,' the later being a play for adults only which set all of London talking.

Summer season concerts came back to The Lawn in 1948, with Sandy Sandford (of Variety Band-Box fame) presenting 'Showtime.' Later in the year, with The Lawn Pavilion now announced as being fully centrally heated, Saturday night in October were reported as fast becoming a pleasant and cosy rendezvous for the many patrons who like a variety entertainment and, more importantly, clean humour, something which is sadly lacking in much of the so-called comedy offered to the public to-day.

In January 1949, The Lawn presented its first-ever professional pantomime, with Sandy Sandford causing much merriment as Widow Twanky in "Aladdin," and Harry Tate Jnr. as Abenazer, the life and soul of the show. He also played golf as part of his turns. Notwithstanding the smallness of the stage, the wonderful scenery and a large cast who all contributed their full share towards the fun, made the pantomime into a really excellent show.

The London Minerva Marionettes opened the summer season in 1949 before a crowded audience and with Richard Murdoch, Kenneth Horne and Maurice Denham being present to wish success to the Marionettes. As something of a novelty in Tankerton, the marvellously clever entertainment proved to be a big success. The year ended with another spectacular pantomime being presented by Sandy Sandford, "Babes in the Wood."

In June 1950 The Lawn was taken over by Miss Beatrice Norledge and her brother Mr. Philip Norledge, who between them had some thirty years experience in the theatre. The theatre was completely redecorated and new seating installed, and opened under the new management on the 16th October, with The Renaissance Players presenting Lady Windemere's Fan.

The Lawn continued with plays and variety for a few more years before being acquired by Dunelm School as their Hall Annex, but by 1960 it was no longer in use. Then, in July 1961 a mystery blaze severely damaged The Lawn. Whitstable firemen turrned two jets on the blaze, which destroyed the whole back part of the roof and damaged about 30 per cent, of the building. Over 100 tip-up seats stored in a corrugated iron shed were also damaged.

Cleared away of the fire damage, the space later served as a fenced-off picnic area and children's playground; facilities that were popular with customers of the adjacent Tankerton Hotel just across the road. Following the eventual closure of the hotel, the site reverted back to a grass extension of the Tankerton slopes — where it had all started some 60 years before.

A WELL-BUILT AND ROOMY HALL FOR VARIETY THEATRE IN SEASALTER

As a small Kent town located by the sea on the Swale estuary, facing the Isle of Sheppey, and sandwiched between Faversham and Whitstable, Seasalter began raising funds in 1902 for the building of its very own town hall or venue that could be used not only for variety and smoking concerts, public and association meetings, dancing, whist drives and local shows but also, according to the church, 'for the deepening of spiritual life.'

Tenders for the building of the hall were opened on the 4th August, 1905, and ranged between £2,307 and £2,982. The contract was eventually awarded to Messrs. Amos and Foad, who had submitted the lowest tender. The foundation stone for the new building, designated Seasalter Parish Hall, was laid on Wednesday November

The Seasalter Parish Hall taken from an old postcard of 1906

189

25th, 1905.

The weather on the day was said to be all that could be desired for the occasion. Early in the morning of the ceremony the coastguards decorated a platform set up in front of the building structure. It was reported that the decorations were so lavish that a stranger might have thought that Royalty was expected — and so it was for the 'Royalty' of the Seasalter cause.

Less than a year later, on Wednesday 25th April, 1906, the opening ceremony of the long wanted Seasalter Parish Hall, a well-built and roomy structure and located on Oxford Street in Whitstable, took place. At four o'clock a short service commenced at the church, the building reported as being well filled. The clergy present were the Rev. T. Pitman (Vicar of Seasalter), Rev. J. H. Martin (Vicar of Whltstable), Rev. T. B. Watkins (Vlcar of Herne Bay), Rev. W, Blissard, Rev. W. Carus Wilson, and the Rev. T. 0. Cross (Faversham). The processional hymn, "Onward, Christian Soldiers," was said to be sung with great fervour, after which evensong was sung, special prayers being read by the Vicar. Following the opening ceremony, teas were served for the assembled gathering inside the Hall.

Almost immediately after the opening of the new Hall, it began to be regularly used for all kinds of events, activities and entertainments. Whist drives became popular, some Parish Council meetings were held in the Hall, while the Kent Coroner conducted some of his inquests there. A Grand Evening Concert was held just a few weeks after the opening ceremony, and Concerts were soon being given by the Whitstable String Band, supported by well-known artistes.

Others frequenting the Hall included the Whitstable Orchestral Society, who used it for rehearsals and concerts, the Whitstable Yacht Club held their Annual Dinner there, and various smoking concerts and gymnastic displays were arranged.

By the end of 1906 a brand new Whitstable Dramatic Club had been formed, using the Hall for rehearsals. Their first ever public concert took place on January 16th, 1907, in a performance of the kind rarely ever seen in Whitstable before. Long before the show was due to begin the seats that were not already booked had all been taken, and standing room only was the word passed to nearly a hundred disappointed applicants waiting outside. The programme provided was one of such exceptional merit that the people who were successful in getting places must have thought themselves lucky.

Mr. Jack Sales, the founder of the Seasalter Dramatic Club, was thanked for his tremendous energy in getting up the entertainment, which included orchestral music, dances, recitations (including 'How old Thomas Pattle very nearly cooked his goose'), piano solos, unique whistling scenes — such as never before seen in Whitstable — a violin solo, and a short farce. This was really the beginning of variety theatre in Whitstable.

Following previous appearances at venues in Faversham, Charles Kay (The well-known London Comedian), together with Miss Nettie Franklin, Mrs Dodman, and the Whitstable String Band, are reported in The *Whitstable Times and Herne Bay Herald* of November 14th, 1908, of being in a concert presented in the Parish Hall by the Seasalter Amateur Dramatic Society.

The following month, in December 1908, the Rev. T. Pitman held

SEASALTER
AMATEUR DRAMATIC SOCIETY,
A CONCERT
Will be given by the above Society on
Wednesday, Nov. 18ᵗʰ, 1906
In
SERASALTER PARISH HALL
Artists:
Miss NETTIE FRANKLIN, R.A.N.
(Gold Medallist)
Miss A. H. DODMAN, L.R.A.N.
Mr CHARLES KAY
(The well known London Comedian)
Mrs FRANK REEVES
The Whitstable String Band under the
conductorship of Mr. J. J. Hill

Exract from an advert in The Whitstable Times and Herne Bay Herald, November 14th 1908. Newspaper image © The British Library Board. All rights reserved. With thanks to The British Newspaper Archive (www.britishnewspaperarchive.co.uk).

his second men's concert for the season at the Parish Hall. Despite other attractions the attendance was excellent. The chairman for the evening was Mr. Charles Kay (making another appearance in Seasalter), Mr. Stanley Anderson acting as vice-chairman. An excellent and varied programme was rendered. Mr. Porter gave two recitations: Mr. Sidney Foad, a promising humorist, secured encores on both occasions; Mr. 0. Saunder's gramophone selections were well received: Mr. John Smith was in good voice; Mr. Taylor, a veteran contributor, had a rousing reception; Mr. Frank Tilley was encored for "Thora," and gave a pretty mandoline solo; the Rev. T. Pitman rendered a lively pianoforte solo; and Mr. Charles Kay, who is 'decidedly one of the most popular comedians who has ever visited Whitstable' provided the "star" turn and rendered four of his funny efforts, teeming with topical and local allusions.' Mr. I. Powell presided at the piano.

This successful concert was to be followed in January 1909 by another concert that was again well received by an appreciative audience, including most of the local leading residents. The presentation of "Alice in Wonderland" proved to be both amusing and puzzling, and the various scenes were sustained with spirit and distinctness. The music, songs, and recitations were said to be certainly well chosen and executed with taste and feeling.

A report on the Seasalter Parish Hall in *The Stage Yearbook* in 1910 indicated that it was 'a modern building, frequently used for concerts.' It went on to state that 'Whitstable has a very fair share of visitors during its season, but these in fine weather seem mainly to patronise alfresco entertainments. During the winter months the hall does well during short engagements. Wednesday is the closing day for the shopkeepers, and that evening and Saturday form the most likely for a full house. Variety entertainments are as a rule much better patronised than dramatic.'

In May 1911 it was reported that Messrs. Maxfield and Day had graciously promised to forego their Animated Picture Entertainment evening to enable a Grand Concert evening to be given on Wednesday 10th May, the object of which was to supply an Ambulance Litter for the Seasalter and Whitstable Ambulance Brigade (under the auspices of the St. John's Ambulance Association).

THE WAR YEARS AND Y.M.C.A ENTERTAINMENT

Concerts, entertainment, shows, dances, whist drives and much more continued as normal at the Seasalter Parish Hall until the outbreak of war in 1914. Now, the Hall began to be utilised for ever more war-related activities. November 1914 sees the Hall being used for a meeting of Special Constables in a scheme approved by the

War Office that provided for compulsory powers for swearing in constables, and in regard to their duties.

In the same month another meeting was held at the Hall, this time to form a local Volunteer Training Corp. and provide training necessary for those who wished to assist the military in the defence of the district. The War Office at this time had issued an order to training camps to revert to the simple company drills outlined in the 1905 book, under which they would have to learn how to fire a rifle.

Volunteers, it was explained, would have read in the papers that the country was up against a foe equipped as no foe had ever been before. It was stated that of the large countries engaged in the war, England was the only one at present that had not been invaded. The volunteers in the Hall were told they needed to be ready to do their duty. It was noted that the Parish Hall was offered free for training, although the Volunteer Corp. would have to pay a reasonable charge for heating and lighting.

By the second year of the war the Y.M.C.A., which undertook grand work among the soldiers all over the country — and now including Whitstable — had leased the Seasalter Parish Hall for the purpose of providing entertainment for the men billeted in the town. The project had a good "send off" by the Chairman of the Urban District Council (Mr. A. W. Daniels, J.P.) and other representative townspeople at the meeting.

One of the regular amateur touring parties "The Entente Cordiale" gave an opening concert in the Seasalter Parish Hall the following Monday evening, which was greatly enjoyed. Captain Kemp presided, and in a short speech, declared the Y.M.C.A. Hall open. Other officers were also present. At the closing of the concert it was announced that throughout the winter other concert parties would be visiting the hall to entertain the men. It was also announced that the Seasalter Hall would in future be open all day, every day, for the use of sailors and soldiers, with every provision being made for the entertainment of the men.

Some of the more notable entertainment at the Hall over the next couple of years included a Fairy Operetta, entitled "The Dream Lady 2," which was advertised as having a chorus of fairies. The entertainment was used to raise funds for further Y.M.C.A concerts.

In Dec 1917 an excellent show devoted to soldiers everywhere was put on for a crowded and enthusiastic audience in the Hall. Songs sung during the evening included "The Golliwogs Duet," "Gilbert the Filbert," "The Night when the Old Cow Died," "Mighty Like a Rose," and the ever-popular "If You Were the Only Girl in the World"

The following year, in December1918 a Grand Annual Concert in aid of the entertainment fund for local troops and wounded was presented at the Hall. Special engagement was made of R.A.F. (Canterbury). in the concert programme entitled the "Spare Parts Pierrots"

By the later part of 1919 the Y.M.C.A. had moved out of the Seasalter Parish Hall and it was returned to the local community to begin organising and presenting the kind of activities, concerts, variety shows, dancing, whist drives, etc., that had been seen there prior to the war.

It was therefore not too long, in November 1919, before the Whitstable Amateur Operatic and Dramatic Society commenced their rehearsals, initially using the Minor Hall in the Seasalter Parish Hall. The first post-war operatic production to be held in the Hall was Gilbert and Sullivan's "Trial by Jury," with Mr. A. Harrison as the musical director.

A VARIED PROGRAMME OF ACTIVITIES RETURNS IN THE 1920S

Into the 1920s, and the Seasalter Parish Hall continues with its varied programme of activities, from concerts, drama, opera, public meeting and, something that seems to particularly appeal to Seasalter and Whitstable residents, Illustrated Lectures. These had been undertaken by well-known historians and public speakers at the Hall for many years. Post war, there were also opportunities for topics related to the war and army or navy life.

The Whitstable Operatic and Dramatic Society is once again performing in early January 1920, producing Gilbert and Sullivan's dramatic cantata "Trial by Jury," as well as a One-Act Comedy entitled "Five Birds in a Cage" and a One-Act play entitled "The Ghost of Jerry Bundler." Later in the month a Grand Concert is given by the celebrated Canterbury Male Voice Choir.

January 1920 also brings a Grand Illustrated Lecture to the Hall, given by a five-year serving territorial entitled "With the Territorials in India," which was supported by over 100 magnificent photographs of the places they visited and the people they met, including scenes from the North-West Frontier and Burma. Other lecture topics at the Hall in the 1920s included "Recent Discoveries in Egypt," "Palestine and Mesoptamia," and a large gathering that assembled to hear of the work of three young lady missionaries in Nigeria.

The following year, in October 1921, the Parish Hall is favoured by a Lantern Address under the auspices of the County of Kent Navy League by no less a person than Rear-Admiral R. A. Hopwood, C.B. entitled "Drake and the New World." The Chairman for the meeting was The Lord Northbourne.

Dramatic and comedy plays, long a staple in previous years, continued well into the 1920s. A special visit by Mr. John Duxbury in November 1920 brought "A Christmas Carol" to the Hall. A big hit of the 1922 season at Seasalter Parish Hall was the presentation of "A Country Girl." The following year Mr Howard Watson presented Mr. J. W. Ellis' comedy in three acts entitles "A Little bit of Fluff." This comedy included the assistance of local well-know local amateurs.

The Whitstable Amateur Operatic Society are back again in April 1923 with a presentation of the famous Dutch Musical Comedy "Miss Hook of Holland," with a full chorus of market folk, soldiers, cheese merchants, villagers and assistants in the liqueur distillery,

THE NAVY LEAGUE.

Seasalter Parish Hall,
WHITSTABLE.

A LANTERN ADDRESS
entitled

"Drake & The New World"

(Under the auspices of the County of Kent Navy League),

will be delivered by

Rear-Admiral R. A. Hopwood, C.B.,
General Secretary of the Navy League, on

THURSDAY, OCTOBER 6th, 1921,
At 7 p.m.

Chairman : THE LORD NORTHBOURNE.

Tickets, Reserved 2/6, Front Seats 2/-, Admission 1/-, to be obtained at the " Whitstable Times " Office, High Street, Whitstable, where plan of the hall can be seen.

HENRY THOMPSON,
Organising Secretary, County of Kent Navy League,
1, Woodstock Road, Strood, Kent.

One of the many lectures to be given at the Seasalter Parish Hall. Reproduced by permission. The Whitstable Times and Tankerton Press. Saturday September 24th, 1921 and dancing by Mddle. Josephine Bruneel.

A first visit to Whitstable and the Seasalater Parish Hall of the "Black and Red Pierrots" occurred in November 1924. The Whitstable Amateur Dramatic and Operatic Society presented "Oh Susannah," a farce in three acts during February 1925.

Great interest was said to be aroused locally when, under the auspices of the Kent County Council, the British Social Hygiene Council arranged a showing of Morality Films at the Seasalter Parish Hall in November 1930. A meeting for women only was held on the Tuesday afternoon when a short address was given by Miss Swaziland. This was followed by the film "The Irresponsibles." Never seen before in Whitstable, the film attracted considerable attention.

The Hall was also used periodically in the 1930s for demonstrations to be held by Spirella, the manufacturers of made-to-measure individually fitted figure training and supporting corsets. The company's products were not sold in shops, but female employees called corsetiers went out to see customers in their homes. Invitation cards for the demonstrations were available from the town's resident corsetiere.

A specially organised great fun day for local children in July 1938 brought performances by the "Great Chinese Conjuring Fantasy" to the Seasalter Hall, with Chin Chin Chinaman providing 100s of laughs and heaps of mysteries to keep the children amused.

ENTERTAINMENT FOR THE FORCES

With the outbreak of war again, the first of a series of dance-socials organised by the Whitstable and Tankerton Townswomen's Guild for the entertainment of members of H.M. Forces was held at

198

the Seasalter Parish Hall in September 1940. Despite a somewhat delayed start due to the unwelcome attention of enemy airoplanes, a full programme of dances, games and musical items was enjoyed and voted a complete success by the assembly.

Dance music for the evening was provided by Mrs. J. Green and a Pte. Popouv, A.M.P.C., one of Czech allies stationed locally, while accordion entertainment was given during the interval by Messrs. Packman and Pattenden, who had formerly played in Charlie Hunt's well-known orchestra. Their lively rendering of popular modern tunes was received with enthusiastic applause. About one quarter of the assembled guests were members the Forces.

Following the end of the war in 1946, a Victory Week Celebration at the Parish Hall saw

SEASALTER PARISH HALL
HIGH STREET, WHITSTABLE
August 12th, 1946 for Six Nights
at 7.30 p.m. and
Matinee Thursday, August 15th at 3 p.m.

AUDREY GARNET present
"THE GAY GARNETS"
As played at the Herne Bay Pier Pavilion during Victory Week Celebrations.

Boys and Girls of sparkling talent and personality in Sketches, Monologues, spectacular Dancing, Singing and Comedy.
The talented Company includes
TREFOR EVANS as COMPERE
(The 14 year old Boy Film Star)
FRED HUDSON ("Albert" in the "Just William" Series, B.B.C.)
THE SIX GLAMOUR GIRLS
RITA LESLEY, TRIXIE, DAWN, JOAN and DIANA
LITTLE BERYL—Tap Specialist
Guest Artiste—**JEAN HUNTER**—Comedienne
AND
"APRIL and JUNE" The Wonder Babes and their amazing Speciality Adagio Act
Admission — 2 6, 1 6 and 1/- including Tax
Children (accompanied by an adult) 1/3, 1/- and 9d
Box Office open at the Hall from 10 a.m. till 4 p.m. daily

The Gay Garnets at Seasalter during Victory Week. Reproduced by permission. The Whitstable times and Tankerton Press. August 10th 1946.

Audrey Garnet present "The Gay Garnets" in which boys and girls of sparkling talent and personality provided sketches, monologues, dancing, singing and comedy. The talented company included Trefor Evans (the 14-year-old boy film star) as the compère, Fred Hudson (Albert in the B.B.C. Just William series), the Six Glamour Girls, and the Wonder Babes with their amazing speciality adagio act.

The Gay Garnets were back again in Seasalter the following

year by popular request and following a vote that had placed the talented company of juvenile stars amongst the cleverest children ever grouped together in one company.

By the end of the 1940s the advent of films had seen variety theatre largely disappearing, leaving the Seasalter Parish Hall as a venue primarily used by local organisation for dances, lectures, whist drives, meetings, film showings, training, and much more.

Today, the Hall, which is leased from the Council, has been in use for more than 30 years as the Whitstable Umbrella Community Centre, a charity community asset managed by a group of Trustees. Whilst receiving some support from the council by way of a rent concession it is now largely self-funded, from hire of rooms, with occasional grant support.

The Hall, and smaller rooms, can be hired for one-off events or on a regular basis for clubs and groups. From Farmers' Markets to yoga classes, live music events and even wrestling the Hall continually strives to nurture and support local charitable activities by providing spaces for free or at a discounted rate. It's not just a venue today but a social hub where it is possible to learn new skills, keep fit, access support and make new friends.

It is also one of the very few theatres and halls built in the second half of the 1800s and early 1900s to provide music hall and variety theatre shows that has not been demolished and turned into flats, shops or offices.

APPENDIX I.
ARTISTES AND ACTS THAT PERFORMED IN KENT'S MUSIC HALLS AND VARIETY THEATRES

The artistes and acts that appeared at Kent's seaside theatres ranged from the country's leading male and female stars, such as Dan Leno and Marie Lloyd, to the many hundreds of nationally lesser-known, more regional and supporting acts that travelled around from one coastal theatre to another throughout the summer season, or participated in touring pantomimes.

Artistes and acts mentioned in the pages of this book are listed below in alphabetical order under the names they were billed by in local newspaper advertisements and on theatre playbills.

A

Albert Grant

Albert Whelan

Ahrensmeyer

Alf Baker

Alf Cawthorn

Alice Lovenez

Alice Raynor

Alpine Charlie

Anita Marita

Arthur J. Hill

Arthur Lomas

Arthur Roberts

Athelda

Aubrey Hylton

Avlis and Francis

B

Barny Ryan

Beatrice Fielding

Bella White

Belle Green

Bennett and Williams

Bernard & Weston

Bert Morland

Beryl Reid

Billie Barlow

Billy Barton

Billy Cotton

Billy Danvers

Billy Gartel

Billy Kray & Margi Morris

Billy Marsden

Black and Red Pierrots

Boris Hambourg

Brampton Trent

Brothers Avones

Buckingham's Performing Dogs

C

Captain Spalding, the wizard of fire

Captain Woodward's sea lions

Charles Kay

Charles Pastor

Chin Chin Chinaman

Cicely Courtneidge

Clack and Clack

Clara Butt

Corbyn's Dogs

D

Daisy Silcott

Daisy Wood

Dan Leno

Derective Copp

Douglas Leonard

D'Oyly Carte Opera Company

Dr. Holden, the Court Magician

Dr. Walford Bodie

Dugwar

Duval Girls

E

Eddie Bayes

Eddies Ross

E Hayes & Billy 'The horse with the human brain'

E. H. Bostock's Baboons

Ella Shields

Elsie & Doris Waters

Elton and Edwin

Elvie Green

Emily Thorne

Emma Rainbow

Emma Stanley

Ethel Buchanan

Eunice Irving

Evelyn Hughes

Evelyn Laye

F

Fanny Smart

Finlay Dunn

Florence Raymond

Four Delvines

Frederic and Drew

Frederic De Lara

Fred Harrington

Fred Karno

Frank Seymour

Frank Somers

Fred Hudson

G

George Roger

George White

Georgia Minstrels

Gertrude Norman

G. H. Elliott

Ginger the Trained Donkey

Giro and Toni

Glen Alva

Gordon Terry, New Zealand's Singing Vagabond

Grannie Pickford

Gurney Russell

H

Hall and Wilson Trio

Hamilton Conrad's Pigeons

Harry Tate Jnr.

Harry Aldridge

Harry Baldwin

Harry Hemsley

Harry Hollis

Harry Randall

Harry Symonds

Harry Wenburn

Hedda Hirleman

Hemsley and Ambrose

Herr Meyer Lutz

Howlett's Marionettes

Hughie Green

I

Iris Sadler

J

Jack Daw

Jack G. Silvano

Jack Hulbert

Jack Hylton

Jane Wood

Jan Hambro

J. C. Crawley

Jen Asta

Jimmy Wood

Joan Dan

Joe Belmont, the Human Bird

Joe Cookson

John Holmes, the Negro comedian

Johnson Troupe

Jolly John Nash

J. P. Boston

Julia Gilbert

K

Kate Williams

Kellino Troupe of Acrobats

Kitty Lofthus

Kubelik

L

La Belle Electra

La Sarella

Lea Davis

Leon & Noel

Leoni Clarke

Leoville

Les Dominos Noirs

Les Hale

Lew Lake

Li Chang Hi

Liege's Monkey Hippodrome

Lil Elfrida

Lillian Troup

Lillie Langtry

Lily Sharplin

Little Dando

Little Miriam Stuart

Lola Trent

Louis Valentine

M

Madan Emma Nevada

Madam Kolman

Mademoiselle Mona Connor

Madge Kellie

Madge Lessing

Marie Blanche

Marie Blythe

Marie Brema

Marie Lloyd

May Dalton

Maud Allen

Maude Rochez's performing monkeys

Maude Wood

Maureen Comfort

Max Miller

Maymo, the Burmese elephant

May Poulton

Mendel, the blind Paderewski

Merry Madge Kelly

Minerva Marionettes

Minnie Letta's Sporting Girls

Miss Le Compt

Mollie Verrell

Moore and Burgess Minstrels

Mons Remo

Monsewer Eddie Gray

Monsieur Le Garcian

N

Nellie Beresford

Nellie Cortine

Nellie Gelton

Nellie Wallace

Netta Conroy

Nettie Franklin

Norman Harper

Norman M. Lee

O

Ottway and Ward

P

Pat O'Brien

Paul Cinqevalli

Paul Robeson

Peels and Curtiss

Percy Emery's Sketch Company

Percy E. Wright

Peter Sellers

Phil Reymond

Prof. Garford and his Troupe of Educated Pigeons

Professor Ernest, the human archestra

Professor Howlett's Royal Marionetten Theatre

Professor Val Miller

Pruno's Unrideable & Uneducated Donkey

Q

Queenie Leighton

R

Rabbits the Clown

Randolph Sutton

Ray Glynne

Renée Reel

R. F. Knox

Roberta Dexter

Rochefort

Russian Kossak Dancers

S

Sailor Baylie

Sandy M'Gregor

Sandy Powell

Sandy Sandford

Sarah Bernhardt

Sarah Thorne

Shamus & Kittie

Sid Field

Singing Blacksmiths

Sisters Archer

Sisters Blemont

Sisters Slater

Sic Brothers Luck

Spangallette and the Joy Wheel Dogs

Squibs

Stylo

Sybil Franklin

Sydney Wood

T

Takio

Talberto and Douglas

Techow's Cats

Teddy

The Almas

The Aza Brothers

The Bohemians

The Brothers Vercells

The Clancy Girls

The Commuters

The Dagonets

The Davenports

The Dolly Girls & Ethel

The Dominoes

The Emerald Girls

The Falconer Sketch Combination

The Faust Brothers

The Five X Rays

The Follies

The Forders and their Lilliputian Stars

The Frassettis

The Gay Garnets

The Gladwells

The Great Cosmo

The Great Levante's Electric Cannon

The Great Platter

The Hall and Wilson Trio

The Jamaica Choir

The Jollity Boys

The Langfords

The Lintons

The Lorettes

The Mascots

The Moore & Burgess Minstrels

The Musical Bon-Bons

The Novelty Bon

The Six Glamour Girls

The Sparkling Mazelles

The Tiller Troupe

The Three Guitanos

The Two Earles

The Two Sordinis

The White Coons

'Tomato' the Educated Donkey

Tom Carney

Tom Delaware

Tom Fancourt

Tommy Banks

Tommy the Wolf

Tommy Trinder

Tom Parker

Tom Wheatley

Tony Gerrard

Topsy Levane

Turkish Tom Thumb

V

Vera Dalwood

Victoria Dagmar

Victoria Monks

Violet Gibson's Tudor Girls

Violet Mills

Viva Daron

Vivian Blanchard

Volcano

W

Walter Macnamara

Wee Georgie Wood

W. Howell Poole

Will English

Will Cruikshanks

Will Powell

Woodhead, the Musical Marvel

W. S. Gilbert Opera Co.

Y

Yuma the Automaton

APPENDIX II.
PANTOMIMES THAT WERE PERFORMED IN KENT'S MUSIC HALLS AND VARIETY THEATRES

Pantomimes were a key element of Kent's seaside music halls and theatres as far back as the middle 1800s. Many took place in early January, or toured for five to ten days from one theatre to another during a pantomime season that sometimes lasted from November to March.

An interesting feature of 19th century pantomimes was that they were not only presented during the Christmas season – as they are today – but that there were also spring pantomimes at Easter-time, such as Goody Two-Shoes, The Home of the Fairies, and Blue Beard, that were often rather more slapstick or comedic in content.

The list below gives an indication of the winter and spring pantomimes mentioned in this publication. Many of course were presented multiple times at different theatres over the course of the 80 to 100 years covered in the book.

Aladdin and the Forty Thieves

Alice in Wonderland

Babes in the Wood

Beauty and the Beast

Blue Beard

Cinderella

Dick Whittington and his Cat

Goody Two-Shoes

Jack and the Beanstalk

Little Red Riding Hood

Mother Goose

Puss in Boots

Robinson Crusoe

Sinbad the Sailor

Snow White

The Home of the Fairies

The Man in the Moon

The Sleeping Beauty

ACKNOWLEDGEMENTS

To be able to research and write a book covering the history and evolution of ten of Kent's music hall and variety theatres – from their very first opening in the middle 19th or early 20th century to their, more recent, eventual closure and demolition – as well as look at and mention many of the hundreds of well-known and lesser performers and acts that visited them, has taken many hours and days studying on-line page archives of Kent's local newspaper, as well as stage and theatre newspapers, that are all now available for researching to subscribers to the British Newspaper Archive.

Acknowledgement and thanks are due to this invaluable resource, particularly for their permission, together with Find My Past and Mirrorpix/Reach Licensing, to reproduce images of Kent theatre and some other local advertisements in the book.

Other resources used for illustrations of Kent theatres, historical music hall and variety artists that performed in Kent, as well old theatre posters, include Alamy, Cairns Collections, Trevor Edwards, the Davenport Collection, Dover and Ramsgate Libraries, The Isle of Thanet News, all of which are again gratefully acknowledged.

ABOUT THE AUTHOR

Michael Fairley has written or contributed to some 30 books in his forty-five year career as a writer, author and publisher, including eight historical or biographical titles, five international encyclopedias and some 15 text or technical books. He has also contributed to magazines and journals worldwide.

Other historical or biographical titles by Michael Fairley that may be of interest to readers are:

■ **Bobbing – Two Thousand Years of Kentish History**

Available from Sittingbourne Heritage Museum

■ **One of life's great charmers.**

A biography of Charles Kay

Sporting legend, songwriter and well-love comedian.

Available through Amazon Books

■ **William Kay**

Cotton manufacturer and liberal benefactor 1775 - 1846

Available through Amazon Books

■ **Diary of the Air Battle over Sittingbourne and Sheppey.**

September 1939 - September 1941

Available from Sittingbourne Heritage Museum

■ **A woman of Power and Influence.**

Herleva de Falaise

From commoner to mother of a king

Available through Amazon Books